Jan Tilley

Jan Tilley is a national leader in nutrition consulting, dietary wellness and weight management. As a registered dietitian, Jan helps at risk clients develop healthy lifestyle alternatives to combat health related issues like type 2 diabetes, heart disease, peri- and post-menopausal symptoms, gastrointestinal disorders and dietary related fatigue and stress. Holding a MS in Nutrition and having over 20 years of experience in the food and nutrition industry working with companies like HEB Grocery, United Supermarkets, Republic Beverage and Methodist Hospital, Jan uses her knowledge of food, nutrition and culinary expertise to provide individual and group weight management, fitness and wellness counseling.

Jan has developed hundreds of nutritious recipes and has incorporated them into three cookbooks. In addition, she authored *Getting Your Second Wind* outlining a path to wellness through physical activity and healthy eating. *Getting Your Second Wind* has given thousands of individuals a fresh start toward creating a positive attitude and balanced lifestyle.

Jan is a highly recommended clinician, nutrition expert, corporate health and wellness expert and motivational speaker. Jan is a member and has served in leadership roles with the Texas Diabetes Council, and the American and Texas Dietetic Associations. Jan served as the Director of the Dietetic Internship program at The University of the Incarnate Word and has served on the Advisory Council of the Food Marketing Institute. Jan speaks nationally on the topic of health and wellness. She also serves as a consultant to premiere food and beverage companies throughout the U.S.

Jan Tilley

Recipe Index

Salads
1

Cashew Chicken
Soba Salad
2

Chicken, Avocado,
& Mango Salad
3

Chinese Chicken Salad
4

Frozen Fruit Salad
5

Fruited Chicken Salad
6

Italian House Salad
7

Pistachio-Crusted
Chicken On Fresh
Field Greens
8

Salmon Salad
9

Shrimp & Pasta Salad
10

Spinach Salad With
Orange Balsamic
Vinaigrette
11

Strawberry
Mediterranean Salad
12

Sunflower
Spinach Salad
13

Soups & Stews
15

5 Hour Stew
16

Chicken Enchilada
Soup
17

Crock-Pot Jambalaya
18

Green Chile Stew
19

Homestyle Chicken
Noodle Soup
20

Souper Easy
Tortilla Soup
21

Southwestern Pork
And Vegetable Stew
22

White Lightening
Texas Chili
23

Beef
25

20-Minute Enchiladas
26

Best Ever Beef Brisket
27

Cornbread Bean
Casserole
28

Easy Skillet Tacos
29

Old-Fashioned
Meatloaf
30

Salisbury Steak
31

Simple Beef Stroganoff
32

Slow-Cooker Pot Roast
33

Spicy Orange Beef
Stir Fry
34

Texas Beef Skillet
35

Chicken
37

Chicken Divan
38

Chicken Pot Pie
39

Chicken With
Snow Peas
40

Cornflake Chicken
41

Easy Chicken
& Dumplings
42

Enchiladas Verdes
43

Honey-Pecan Chicken
44

Jalapeno Orange
Chicken
45

Jan's Chicken
46

Lemon-Spinach
Chicken
47

Mexican Spaghetti
48

Szechuan Chicken
With Angel Hair Pasta
49

Pork
51

Grilled Jalapeno-Basil
Pork Chops
52

Ham & Swiss Capellini
With Mushrooms
53

Molasses-Grilled
Pork Tenderloin
54

Pork Chalupas
55

Pork Chops With
Apple Pilaf
56

Slow Cooker Root
Beer Pulled Pork
57

Smothered Pork
Chops
58

Swedish Pork Chops
With Sour Cream
Sauce
59

Seafood
61

Cajun Shrimp Pasta
62

Crispy Baked Tilapia
63

One-Pot Shrimp Paella
64

Pan Roasted Salmon With Tomato-Citrus Salsa
65

Salmon With Brown Sugar Mustard Glaze
66

Sesame Shrimp Stir-Fry
67

Shrimp Boil Hobo Dinners
68

Spicy Lemon Tilapia
69

Vegetarian
71

Black Bean Skillet Dinner
72

Huevos Rancheros
73

Penne Pasta With Asparagus & Toasted Pecans
74

Penne Pasta With Tomato Cream
75

Spinach Lasagna
76

Vegetable Frittata
77

Vegetable Quesadillas
78

Vegetarian Supper
79

Sandwiches
81

Barbequed Salmon Sandwiches
82

Chicken Lettuce Wraps
83

French Dip Sandwiches
84

Green Chili Cheeseburgers
85

Hawaiian Chicken Sandwiches
86

Lazy Day Barbeque Sandwiches
87

Peanut Chicken Pitas
88

Southwest Beef Wraps
89

Tuna Club Sandwiches
90

Turkey Avocado Pinwheels
91

Side Dishes
93

Caramelized Cauliflower
94

Cheesy Grilled Potato Packets
95

Fresh Tomato & Squash Tart
96

Glazed Sweet Potatoes With Cranberries
97

Mashed Maple Sweet Potatoes
98

Mexican Squash
99

Roasted Fresh Asparagus
100

Zucchini Au Gratin
101

Desserts & Snacks
103

All-Bran Muffins
104

Bird's Nests
105

Blackberry Apple Crisp With Nut Topping
106

Cherry Crunch Parfaits
107

Magic Cherry Cobbler
108

"No-Cook" Banana Pudding
109

Pineapple Angel Cake
110

Spicy Nut Popcorn
111

Strawberry Angel Pie
112

Strawberry Fluff
113

Sunkist Sherbet
114

Chicken, Avocado, & Mango Salad, p. 3

Salads

Salads are an easy way to get a variety of fresh produce in one dish. The more color you add to your salad, the richer it will be in 'good for you' nutrients!

The salads I've included for you provide a combination of fruits, vegetables, protein, and healthy fat, which make them a great side dish or complete meal! Salads are a great source of insoluble and soluble fiber, which comes from fruit, vegetables, beans and whole wheat pasta. Insoluble fiber is important for regulating your digestive system and helps keep you feeling full longer. Soluble fiber forms a gelatinous substance that helps manage cholesterol and glucose. I tell my patients soluble fiber is a magical substance that can work to control and even reverse their elevated cholesterol and glucose levels – use it to eat your way back to good health!

As we all know, the most dangerous part of a salad is the dressing! It can be loaded with fat and calories and sabotage all the good you are doing by choosing salad over a heavier meal. One of my favorite tricks for using less salad dressing is to put all the salad fixings in a large bowl, drizzle on two tablespoons of salad dressing, and toss it really well. It coats all the veggies and makes less dressing seem like more!

Did you know...

- One cup of raw vegetables has only 25 calories!
- Find a reduced-fat salad dressing you enjoy and use it in moderation – about 2 tablespoons per serving. You can also try using fresh lemon or lime juice – I even like salsa on my salad!

CASHEW CHICKEN SOBA SALAD

Ingredients

3 cups diced Rotisserie chicken or
3 cups diced cooked chicken breast

1 tablespoon rice vinegar

1-½ tablespoons peanut oil

2 teaspoons low-sodium soy sauce

1 teaspoon honey

1 teaspoon chile garlic sauce

½ teaspoon salt

2 cups cooked (about 4 ounces uncooked) soba noodles or whole wheat spaghetti

1 cup grated carrots

¼ cup thinly sliced green onions

¼ cup minced red onion

¼ cup chopped fresh basil

4 teaspoons chopped cashews

4 lime wedges

Directions

1. Shred chicken into large bowl; set aside.

2. In a small bowl, whisk together vinegar, oil, soy sauce, honey, chile garlic sauce and salt. Pour over shredded chicken and let stand 5 minutes. Add soba noodles, carrots, green onions, red onion, fresh basil and toss well.

3. Divide into 4 salad bowls. Top each with 1 teaspoon of chopped cashews, squeeze with lime wedge and serve.

Makes 4 servings

Nutrition Information

320 calories, 9 grams fat, 70 mg cholesterol, 480 mg sodium,
31 grams carbohydrate, 5 grams fiber, 32 grams protein

Exchanges: 2 carbohydrate, 4.5 protein, 2 fat

CHICKEN, AVOCADO, & MANGO SALAD

Ingredients

3 tablespoons fresh lime juice

1 teaspoon sugar

Dash of ground ginger

¼ teaspoon salt

1 tablespoon olive oil

3 tablespoons minced fresh cilantro

8 cups torn romaine lettuce leaves

2 mangos, peeled and diced

3 cups grilled chicken strips

2 small avocados, diced

¼ cup red onion, thinly sliced

Directions

1. In bottom of large bowl, whisk together 2 tablespoons lime juice, sugar, ginger, salt, olive oil and 1 tablespoon minced cilantro; add lettuce; toss well.

2. Arrange dressed greens evenly on platter. Distribute mango, chicken and avocado. Sprinkle with remaining cilantro.

3. Drizzle remaining lime juice. Top with red onion slices. Serve immediately.

   Makes 4 servings

Nutrition Information

280 calories, 9 grams fat, 60 mg cholesterol, 700 mg sodium, 24 grams carbohydrate, 5 grams fiber, 28 grams protein

Exchanges: 1.5 carbohydrate, 4 protein, 2 fat

CHINESE CHICKEN SALAD

Ingredients

1 large head of cabbage, thinly sliced

3 chicken breasts, cooked and diced

1 bell pepper, diced

2 bunches green onions, diced

3 packages chicken flavored
Ramen Noodles, crushed

½ cup slivered almonds, toasted
for 10 minutes at 350 degrees

2 tablespoons sesame seeds, toasted
for 10 minutes at 350 degrees

Dressing:

⅓ cup canola oil

3 packages Ramen chicken flavoring

3 tablespoons vinegar

2 tablespoons sugar

Directions

1. In large bowl, mix together cabbage, chicken, bell pepper, green onions, crushed Ramen noodles, toasted almonds and sesame seeds.

2. In small bowl, whisk together canola oil, Ramen Chicken flavoring, vinegar and sugar. Pour over cabbage mixture; toss well and serve.

   Makes 10 servings

Nutrition Information

310 calories, 16 grams fat, 20 mg cholesterol, 570 mg sodium, 28 grams carbohydrate, 4 grams fiber, 14 grams protein

Exchanges: 2 carbohydrate, 2 protein, 3 fat

FROZEN FRUIT SALAD

Ingredients

1 cup water

¼ cup sugar

10 large marshmallows

2 (10 oz) cartons frozen sweetened sliced strawberries, thawed

1 (15.25 oz) can apricot halves, drained and cut into bite-sized pieces

1 (15.2 oz) can crushed pineapple

4 bananas, sliced

Directions

1. In small saucepan, combine water and sugar. Heat and stir until sugar is dissolved. Add marshmallows and stir until melted; remove from heat.

2. Add remaining ingredients and pour into 9 X 13-inch Pyrex dish and place on flat surface in freezer for at least 6 hours.

3. To serve, cut into squares and serve frozen.

   Makes 12 servings

Nutrition Information

180 calories, 0 grams fat, 0 mg cholesterol, 10 mg sodium, 46 carbohydrate, 4 grams fiber, 1 gram protein

Exchanges: 3 carbohydrate, 0 protein, 0 fat

FRUITED CHICKEN SALAD

Ingredients

¾ cup Miracle Whip Light

¼ cup 1% milk

½ teaspoon seasoned salt

2-½ cups skinless, boneless chicken breasts, cooked and cubed

1-½ cups red grapes, cut in half

1 cup celery, sliced thin

⅓ cup green onions, sliced (optional)

⅓ cup chopped pecans, toasted

6 avocado halves, optional

Directions

1. Combine Miracle Whip, milk and salt; set aside.
2. In a separate bowl, combine remaining ingredients.
3. Pour dressing over chicken mixture and toss gently.
4. Serve on top of avocado halves, if desired.

   Makes 6 servings

Nutrition Information

240 calories, 13 grams fat, 55 mg cholesterol, 440 mg sodium, 14 grams carbohydrate, 2 grams fiber, 13 grams protein

Exchanges: 1 carbohydrate, 2 protein, 2.5 fat

Ingredients

1 large head red leaf lettuce, torn

1 (14 oz) can artichoke heart quarters, drained

1 (6 oz) can pitted ripe olives, drained

4 plum tomatoes, coarsely chopped

1 small red onion, thinly sliced

¼ pound provolone cheese, shredded

Dressing

3 tablespoons shredded Parmesan cheese

⅓ cup canola oil

¼ cup red wine vinegar

1 teaspoon Italian seasoning

1 teaspoon dried parsley

¼ teaspoon garlic powder

¼ teaspoon pepper

⅛ teaspoon salt

Directions

1. In a small bowl, whisk together ingredients for dressing; set aside.
2. Place lettuce and next 5 ingredients in a large bowl.
3. Drizzle with dressing, and gently toss to coat.

   Makes 8 servings

Nutrition Information

170 calories, 13 grams fat, 5 mg cholesterol, 600 mg sodium, 10 grams carbohydrate, 3 grams fiber, 5 grams protein

Exchanges: 0.5 carbohydrate, 1 protein, 2.5 fat

PISTACHIO-CRUSTED CHICKEN ON FRESH FIELD GREENS

Ingredients

¼ cup shelled, finely chopped pistachios

½ cup panko breadcrumbs

½ teaspoon garlic salt

½ teaspoon black pepper

4 (4 oz) skinless, boneless chicken breast halves, pounded to even thickness

1 tablespoon olive oil

4 cups baby spinach leaves

4 cups fresh field greens

1 cup cherry tomatoes, halved

½ avocado, diced

1 yellow bell pepper, cut into thin strips

2 green onions, sliced

2 tablespoons grated Parmesan cheese

¼ cup light balsamic vinaigrette

Directions

1. Mix together chopped pistachios, panko breadcrumbs, garlic salt, and pepper on large plate.

2. Press chicken breasts into the pistachio mixture. Heat oil in oven-proof skillet over medium-high heat, place coated chicken breasts into hot oil and brown on each side. Place into 350 degree oven for about 10 minutes or until cooked through. Remove chicken to cutting board, let cool, and slice into thin strips; set aside.

3. In large bowl, place spinach leaves, field greens, tomatoes, avocado, bell pepper, and green onions. Sprinkle with Parmesan cheese, drizzle with Balsamic vinaigrette and toss well.

4. Divide salad evenly onto 4 plates. Top each with chicken strips and serve.

Makes 4 servings

Nutrition Information

410 calories, 16 grams fat, 90 mg cholesterol, 540 mg sodium, 29 grams carbohydrate, 6 grams fiber, 40 grams protein

Exchanges: 2 carbohydrate, 6 protein, 3 fat

SALMON SALAD

Ingredients

1 (3 oz) packet of salmon

2 tablespoons light Miracle Whip

8 red grapes, quartered

1-2 small dill pickles, diced

½ red pear or apple, diced

½ teaspoon ground black pepper

2 tablespoons sliced almonds

4 cups fresh spinach

Directions

1. Mix all ingredients, except spinach, in medium bowl.
2. May need to add more Miracle Whip or black pepper to taste.
3. Serve in mound over fresh spinach. Sprinkle with additional almonds and red grapes, if desired.

   Makes 2 servings

Nutrition Information

210 calories, 11 grams fat, 30 mg cholesterol, 420 mg sodium,
20 grams carbohydrate, 5 grams fiber, 12 grams protein

Exchanges: 1.5 carbohydrate, 2 protein, 2 fat

SHRIMP & PASTA SALAD

Ingredients

8 oz. uncooked small whole wheat pasta shells

2 pounds small shrimp, cooked and peeled

6 green onions, thinly sliced

½ cup fresh basil, chopped

1 tablespoon grated lemon rind

1-½ teaspoons dried crushed red pepper

Fresh Citrus Salad Dressing

⅓ cup olive oil

3 tablespoons Greek seasoning

3 tablespoons fresh lemon juice

3 tablespoons light mayonnaise

Directions

1. Prepare pasta according to package directions.
2. In small bowl, whisk together ingredients for dressing; set aside.
3. Toss pasta with remaining ingredients and salad dressing. Serve immediately or cover and chill up to 2 days.

   Makes 8 servings

Nutrition Information

340 calories, 13 grams fat, 225 mg cholesterol, 480 mg sodium, 25 grams carbohydrate, 3 grams fiber, 28 grams protein

Exchanges: 1.5 carbohydrate, 4 protein, 2.5 fat

SPINACH SALAD WITH ORANGE BALSAMIC VINAIGRETTE

Ingredients

1 (10 oz) bag baby spinach

1 (10 oz) bag romaine lettuce

¼ small red onion, thinly sliced

⅓ cup reduced-fat feta cheese crumbles

⅓ cup dried cranberries

2 tablespoons toasted sliced almonds

Dressing

½ cup bottled balsamic vinaigrette salad dressing

2 tablespoons orange juice

1 teaspoon orange zest, optional

Directions

1. Place spinach and romaine lettuce in a large serving bowl.

2. Add onion and half of the feta cheese crumbles; toss to combine.

3. Combine dressing ingredients in a small mixing bowl. Pour over salad and toss to coat.

4. Sprinkle with remaining cheese. Top with sweetened dried cranberries and almonds. Serve immediately.

   Makes 4 servings

Nutrition Information

230 calories, 13 grams fat, 10 mg cholesterol, 790 mg sodium, 24 grams carbohydrate, 6 grams fiber, 9 grams protein

Exchanges: 1.5 carbohydrate, 1 protein, 2.5 fat

STRAWBERRY MEDITERRANEAN SALAD

Ingredients

½ pint fresh strawberries, sliced

1 cup fresh mushrooms, sliced

½ cup red bell pepper, julienne sliced

¼ cup green onion, sliced

1 (10 oz) package fresh baby spinach

½ cup walnuts, chopped

⅓ cup reduced-fat
feta cheese crumbles

Dressing

2 tablespoons olive oil

2 tablespoons canola oil

2 tablespoons balsamic vinegar

2 teaspoons water

¼ teaspoon salt

Pepper to taste

Directions

1. Combine salad ingredients except walnuts and feta cheese crumbles; set aside.
2. In medium bowl, whisk together dressing ingredients. Pour over salad, toss, and set aside.
3. Add feta cheese and walnuts as topping and serve.

   Makes 4 servings

Nutrition Information

190 calories, 12 grams fat, 5 mg cholesterol, 650 mg sodium,
21 grams carbohydrate, 6 grams fiber, 9 grams protein

Exchanges: 1.5 carbohydrate, 1 protein, 2 fat

Ingredients

6 cups romaine lettuce, torn

6 cup fresh spinach, torn

½ cup cherry tomatoes, halved

½ cup shredded carrots

4 hard-boiled eggs, sliced

1 (1 oz) slice 2% Swiss cheese,
cut in julienne strips

1 (1 oz) slice low-fat cheddar cheese,
cut in julienne strips

¼ cup sunflower kernels, toasted

½ cup light balsamic vinaigrette salad
dressing

Directions

1. Combine romaine, spinach, tomatoes and carrots in large bowl.
   Toss with salad dressing.

2. Top with egg slices, cheese strips, and sunflower kernels. Toss gently and serve.

   Makes 6 servings

Nutrition Information

120 calories, 7 grams fat, 145 mg cholesterol, 350 mg sodium,
8 grams carbohydrate, 2 grams fiber, 8 grams protein

Exchanges: 0.5 carbohydrate, 1 protein, 1 fat

Southwestern Pork & Vegetable Stew, p. 22

Soups & Stews

There are few things better than a hearty bowl of soup on a cold winter day. Besides keeping you warm, soup has amazing nutritional benefits. The soups and stews I've included for you are hearty and full of nutrients, yet relatively low in calories.

Preparing soups and stews are a great way to use up leftover vegetables (green beans, carrots and squash are delicious additions) and starches (think rice, pasta and potatoes), and proteins (like beef and chicken). Use high flavor liquids to add depth to your soup or stew – like tomato juice, broth and wine. I've included my recipe for *5 Hour Stew* (page 16) which uses V-8 Juice to bring a delicious depth of flavor to this quick-to-fix version of old fashioned beef stew.

If you love cream soups, but don't love the calories, my *Chicken Enchilada Soup* (page 17) is just for you! The secret? The recipe uses light sour cream and light Velveeta in combination with chicken broth to create a velvety smooth texture. Add in the spicy green chilies and you are in for an unbelievable taste treat!

Did you know...

- Soup can also be used as a method for weight management. Several studies confirm that consuming a low-calorie soup before a meal can help reduce your calorie intake at mealtime.
- Canned soups can be extremely high in sodium. Look for "Healthy Request" canned soups, or better still – make your own using low-sodium broth.

5 HOUR STEW

Ingredients

2 pounds rump roast*,
trimmed of all visible fat

2 cups carrots, sliced

2 cups potatoes, cubed

2 cups celery, chopped

2 cups onion, chopped

2 cups V8 juice + 4 cups water

2 tablespoons Worcestershire sauce

2 teaspoons each sugar and salt

2 bay leaves

3 tablespoons minute tapioca

Directions

1. Cut roast into 1-inch cubes.
2. Mix all ingredients together in large oven-proof casserole dish.
3. Bake at 250 degrees for 5 hours. Remove bay leaves and serve.

   Makes 8 servings

Nutrition Information

240 calories, 5 grams fat, 55 mg cholesterol, 820 mg sodium,
23 grams carbohydrate, 3 grams fiber, 25 grams protein

Exchanges: 1.5 carbohydrate, 4 protein, 1 fat

*May use lean stew meat

Ingredients

¼ cup butter

1 large onion, chopped

2 garlic cloves, minced

¼ cup flour

4 (14 oz) cans low sodium chicken broth

1 (4 oz) can green chilies

3 cups cooked chicken, diced*

8 corn tortillas, cut into small pieces

1 (8 oz) package light Velveeta shreds

1 (8 oz) container light sour cream

Directions

1. In large Dutch oven, melt butter. Add onion and garlic; sauté until translucent. Add flour to make a paste; cook for 1 minute.

2. Add chicken broth and green chilies; cook and stir until thickened.

3. Stir in chicken, tortillas, and shredded cheese. Cook over low heat until cheese is melted and tortillas soften.

4. Stir in sour cream. Warm through, but do not boil.

   Makes 8 servings

Nutrition Information

350 calories, 14 grams fat, 85 mg cholesterol, 1010 mg sodium, 24 grams carbohydrate, 2 grams fiber, 32 grams protein

Exchanges: 1.5 carbohydrate, 4 protein, 3 fat

*May use canned premium white meat chicken

CROCK-POT JAMBALAYA

Ingredients

½ pound smoked sausage,
cut into ½ inch slices

½ pound skinless, boneless chicken
breasts, cut into 1-inch cubes

1 (14.5 oz) can chicken broth

1 (14.5 oz) can diced tomatoes

½ cup chopped celery

½ cup chopped onion

4 garlic cloves, minced

2 teaspoons spicy Creole seasoning

1 teaspoon Worcestershire sauce

1 teaspoon Tabasco sauce

2 bay leaves

¾ cup rice, uncooked

1 pound medium shrimp,
peeled and deveined

Directions

1. In crock-pot, combine sausage, chicken, broth, tomatoes, celery, onion, garlic, Creole seasoning, Worcestershire sauce, Tabasco sauce and bay leaves. Cover and cook on low for 7 to 8 hours.

2. Stir in shrimp and rice. Cover and cook 30 minutes or until rice is tender and shrimp is cooked through. Remove bay leaves, adjust seasonings to taste and serve.

Makes 6 servings

Nutrition Information

200 calories, 3 grams fat, 150 mg cholesterol, 1180 mg sodium,
16 grams carbohydrate, 1 gram fiber, 27 grams protein

Exchanges: 1 carbohydrate, 4 protein, 0.5 fat

GREEN CHILE STEW

Ingredients

2 pounds lean beef or pork cut into small cubes

1 small onion, chopped

4 cloves garlic, minced

1 teaspoon ground cumin

1 teaspoon dried oregano

1 teaspoon salt

1 tablespoon canola oil

2 large potatoes, peeled and cut into cubes

1 pound green chiles, roasted, peeled and chopped

3 Roma tomatoes, chopped

4 cups low-sodium beef broth

Corn tortillas, optional

Directions

1. Brown meat, onion, garlic and seasonings in oil in a large stew pot.

2. Add potatoes, chiles, tomatoes and broth, bring to a boil and simmer over low heat for 30 minutes.

3. Serve with warm corn tortillas.

   Makes 10 servings

Nutrition Information

210 calories, 4.5 grams fat, 50 mg cholesterol, 490 mg sodium, 19 grams carbohydrate, 3 grams fiber, 24 grams protein

Exchanges: 1 carbohydrate, 3.5 protein, 1 fat

HOMESTYLE CHICKEN NOODLE SOUP

Ingredients

4 split fryer breasts*

4 carrots

4 celery stalks

1 onion, diced

1 teaspoon seasoned salt

¼ teaspoon pepper

1 (14 oz) can low-sodium chicken broth

3 cups dry egg noodles

Directions

1. Place chicken in a large Dutch oven. Sprinkle with seasonings and place vegetables around the sides of pan.

2. Add 4 cups water, cover and bake at 350 degrees for 1 hour.

3. Remove chicken and vegetables and set aside to cool.

4. Add chicken broth and 1 can of water to pan juices; bring to a boil.

5. Add noodles and boil until tender.

6. Remove skin from chicken, debone and cut into bite-sized pieces; slice vegetables, and add both to noodles.

7. Heat through and serve immediately.

Makes 6 servings

Nutrition Information

360 calories, 11 grams fat, 90 mg cholesterol, 1150 mg sodium, 34 grams carbohydrate, 4 grams fiber, 29 grams protein

Exchanges: 2 carbohydrate, 4 protein, 2 fat

*May use 4 cups of diced Rotisserie Chicken

Ingredients

1 (10 oz) can diced tomatoes with green chilies

3 (10.75 oz) Campbell's Healthy Request Chicken with Rice Soup

1 (9.75 oz) can Swanson Premium White Meat Chicken

1 cup crumbled tortilla chips

1-½ cups low-fat cheddar cheese shreds

Directions

1. Combine tomatoes, soups and chicken in medium sauce pan. Bring to a boil; reduce heat and simmer for 10 minutes.

2. Divide crumbled chips evenly into the bottom of each bowl. Ladle soup over chips and top with cheese.

Makes 6 servings

Nutrition Information

220 calories, 11 grams fat, 40 mg cholesterol, 840 mg sodium, 16 grams carbohydrate, 1 gram fiber, 18 grams protein

Exchanges: 1 carbohydrate, 2.5 protein, 2 fat

SOUTHWESTERN PORK AND VEGETABLE STEW

Ingredients

1 tablespoon olive or canola oil

1 lb pork tenderloin,
cut into ¾-inch pieces

1 medium onion, coarsely chopped

1 clove garlic, finely chopped

1-½ cups red potatoes,
cut into ½-inch pieces

1 cup frozen corn

½ medium red bell pepper,
coarsely chopped

2 cups low-sodium chicken broth

1 can (14.5 oz) white hominy,
drained, rinsed

1 can (4.5 oz) chopped green chilies,
undrained

1 tablespoon chili powder

1 teaspoon dried oregano leaves

1 teaspoon ground cumin

½ teaspoon salt

Directions

1. In 3-quart saucepan or Dutch oven, heat oil over medium-high heat. Add pork;
   cook and stir 3 to 4 minutes or until browned.

2. Add onion and garlic; cook and stir 1 to 2 minutes or until onion is crisp-tender.

3. Stir in remaining ingredients. Heat to boiling. Reduce heat; cover and simmer
   30 minutes, stirring occasionally, until potatoes are tender and pork is no longer
   pink in center.

   Makes 6 servings

Nutrition Information

330 calories, 14 grams fat, 65 mg cholesterol, 680 mg sodium
29 grams carbohydrate, 4 grams fiber, 24 grams protein

Exchanges: 2 carbohydrate, 3.5 protein, 3 fat

WHITE LIGHTENING TEXAS CHILI

You're going to love this one! It takes 5 minutes to put together and a healthy dinner is ready when you get home from work!

Ingredients

4 skinless boneless chicken breasts

2 cups low sodium chicken broth

1 medium onion, chopped

1 (4 oz) can diced green chilies

1 (14.5 oz) can diced tomatoes

1 teaspoon each cumin and garlic salt

½ teaspoon ground oregano

⅛ teaspoon cayenne pepper

2 (16 oz) cans navy beans, drained & rinsed

Optional Toppings: Pepper jack cheese shreds & chopped green onion

Directions

1. Place chicken breasts in bottom of crock pot. Add chicken broth, onion, green chilies, tomatoes, seasonings and cook on low for 4 hours.

2. Add beans and cook additional 2 hours or until ready to serve. Adjust salt to taste.

3. Top each serving with cheese and green onion, if desired.
   Makes 6 servings

Nutrition Information

290 calories, 2.5 grams fat, 45 mg cholesterol, 780 mg sodium, 37 grams carbohydrate, 9 grams fiber, 30 grams protein

Exchanges: 2.5 carbohydrate, 4 protein, 0.5 fat

Spicy Orange Beef Stir Fry, p. 34

Beef

Often people think they should shy away from beef for health reasons, but did you know there is NO REASON to eliminate lean beef from your diet? There are 29 cuts of beef that fit into a healthy diet and meet government guidelines considered 'lean'. These cuts of beef contain less than 10 grams of fat per 3-ounce serving. Use this easy slogan to help you remember how to select lean beef at the grocery store - "if it's round or loin, it's lean!" To include beef as a part of your healthy diet, choose beef cuts such as top round, eye of round, sirloin, tenderloin or extra lean ground beef.

Lean beef is an excellent source of protein, zinc, and phosphorus, as well as a good source of niacin, iron and riboflavin. These nutrients provide important functions such as maintaining optimal immune function, healthy growth, and transporting oxygen throughout the body.

I've included a delicious *Best Ever Beef Brisket* (page 27) recipe, it is mouth-wateringly delicious and when trimmed of all visible fat, brisket is a lean cut of beef. The recipe for *Spicy Orange Beef Stir-Fry* (page 34) has a wonderful fresh taste, is very low in fat, and perfect for that quick-to-fix family meal.

Beef Tip:

- Save money! Next time you need to purchase ground beef for a recipe, buy 80/20, brown it in a skillet, pour into colander, rinse with hot water, pat dry with paper towels and return to skillet. You will reduce the fat content to 95/5 without spending the extra money.
- Remember to watch your portion sizes. The average adult male needs 5 to 6 ounces of protein per meal and the average adult female needs 3 to 4 ounces per meal - most restaurants serve twice that amount!
- Picture this! A deck of cards (size and thickness) is a good way to estimate a 3 ounce serving of meat.

20-MINUTE ENCHILADAS

This sounds strange, but it is one of the best Mexican-style casseroles I've ever had – everyone loves it!

Ingredients

1 pound 95% lean ground beef, browned and drained

1 (10 oz) can diced tomatoes with green chilies

1 (10.75 oz) can Campbell's Healthy Request Cream of Mushroom Soup

1 (15 oz) can lean chili without beans

8 corn tortillas

2 cups reduced-fat cheddar cheese shreds

Directions

1. Combine browned beef, tomatoes, soup, and chili.

2. Spoon 2 cups of meat mixture into greased 9 X 13-inch glass dish. Top with 4 tortillas, torn to cover. Layer half remaining meat mixture and cheese shreds.

3. Top with remaining tortillas, meat mixture and cheese. Bake at 350 degrees for 20 minutes, or until bubbly.

   Makes 8 servings

Nutrition Information

260 calories, 10 grams fat, 50 mg cholesterol, 850 mg sodium, 19 grams carbohydrate, 2 grams fiber, 24 grams protein

Exchanges: 1 carbohydrate, 3.5 protein, 2 fat

Ingredients

6 pound beef brisket, trimmed of all visible fat

1 teaspoon each garlic salt and onion salt

1-½ teaspoon each salt, pepper and celery salt

2 tablespoons Worcestershire sauce

Sauce:

½ cup sugar

1 cup barbecue sauce

1 cup broth (from cooked brisket)

1 cup Wish-Bone Russian Dressing

Directions

1. Mix seasonings and Worcestershire sauce together and rub into meat. Wrap tightly in heavy-duty aluminum foil. Place in 9 X 13-inch Pyrex or roaster. Cook 7 to 8 hours at 275 degrees.

2. Take out of oven, and remove from foil. Reserve 1 cup of broth for sauce; discard remaining broth.

3. Slice and put brisket back in pan.

4. Mix together ingredients for sauce; pour over brisket slices, cover and bake at 300 degrees for 1 hour.

   Makes 12 servings

Nutrition Information

310 calories, 10 grams fat, 95 mg cholesterol, 710 mg sodium, 3 grams carbohydrate, 0 grams fiber, 47 grams protein

Exchanges: 0 carbohydrate, 6.5 protein, 2 fat

CORNBREAD BEAN CASSEROLE

Ingredients

1 pound extra lean ground beef

1 onion, chopped

½ teaspoon salt and pepper

2 tablespoons chili powder

1 teaspoon Worcestershire sauce

¼ teaspoon garlic powder

1 (10.75 oz.) can Campbell's Tomato Soup

1 (15 oz.) can Ranch Style Beans

1 (6 oz.) package cornbread mix

½ cup reduced-fat cheddar cheese shreds

Directions

1. In large skillet, brown meat and onion; drain well. Add salt, pepper, chili powder, Worcestershire sauce, garlic powder, soup and beans. Pour meat mixture into an 8X8-inch square glass baking dish.

2. Mix cornbread as directed on package. Place on top of meat mixture.

3. Bake at 350 degrees for 25 minutes or until cornbread is done. Cover top of cornbread with cheese and return to oven until cheese melts.

   Makes 6 servings

Nutrition Information

400 calories, 11 grams fat, 75 mg cholesterol, 1120 mg sodium, 44 grams carbohydrate, 6 grams fiber, 33 grams protein

Exchanges: 3 carbohydrate, 5 protein, 2 fat

Here is a quick, easy dinner that is ready to serve in 30 minutes - AND your family will love it!!

Ingredients

1 pound extra lean ground beef

½ cup finely chopped onion

1 tablespoon chili powder

1-½ teaspoons ground cumin

1 teaspoon salt

1 (15 oz) can pinto beans, rinsed and drained

1 (8 oz) can tomato sauce

¾ cup water

½ cup salsa

1-½ cups shredded reduced-fat cheddar cheese shreds

1 tablespoon chopped fresh cilantro

12 corn tortillas

Optional toppings: Shredded lettuce, diced tomato, avocado, salsa, & jalapenos

Directions

1. In large skillet, cook ground beef over medium-high heat, stirring until beef crumbles and is no longer pink. Add onion, chili powder, cumin and salt. Cook over low heat, stirring to prevent sticking, for about 10 minutes.

2. Stir in beans, tomato sauce, water, and salsa. Mash pinto beans in skillet with a fork, leaving some beans whole. Bring to a boil; reduce heat and simmer uncovered for 10 minutes or until liquid is reduced.

3. Top evenly with cheese and cilantro. Cover, turn off heat, and let stand 5 minutes or until cheese is melted. Serve with corn tortillas and desired toppings.

Makes 6 servings

Nutrition Information

200 calories, 6 grams fat, 30 mg cholesterol, 570 mg sodium, 22 grams carbohydrate, 3 grams fiber, 14 grams protein

Exchanges: 1.5 carbohydrate, 2 protein, 1 fat

OLD-FASHIONED MEATLOAF

This meatloaf has been perfected over the years and has the best flavor and consistency of any I've ever tasted – it is my husband's favorite meal. It takes a little extra time, but it's worth it!

Ingredients

1 tablespoon butter

3 ribs celery, chopped

½ large onion, chopped

2 pounds lean ground beef

2 tablespoons Worcestershire sauce, divided

½ cup Italian-seasoned bread crumbs

⅓ cup ketchup

1 (8 oz) can tomato sauce; reserving ¼ cup

2 teaspoons Creole seasoning

1 teaspoon Cavender's Greek seasoning

1 teaspoon garlic salt

2 eggs, lightly beaten

3 tablespoons tomato paste

1 tablespoon ketchup

Directions

1. Melt butter in medium skillet; add celery and onion and sauté until just tender.

2. In large bowl, stir together celery mixture, ground beef, 1 tablespoon Worcestershire sauce, breadcrumbs, ketchup and tomato sauce (reserve ¼ cup), and next 4 ingredients.

3. Shape into a 10 x 5-inch loaf pan. Bake at 350 degrees for 45 minutes. Stir together remaining 1 tablespoon Worcestershire sauce, remaining ¼ cup tomato sauce, tomato paste and 1 tablespoon ketchup until blended; pour evenly over meatloaf, and bake 10 to 15 minutes. Let stand for 10 minutes before serving.

Makes 8 servings

Nutrition Information

220 calories, 8 grams fat, 115 mg cholesterol, 940 mg sodium, 13 grams carbohydrate, 1 gram fiber, 25 grams protein

Exchanges: 1 carbohydrate, 3.5 protein, 1.5 fat

Ingredients

1-¼ pounds extra lean ground beef

⅓ cup finely chopped onion

¼ cup saltine cracker crumbs

1 egg, slightly beaten

2 tablespoons 1% milk

¼ teaspoon salt

⅛ teaspoon pepper

1 (.75 oz) mushroom gravy mix

Directions

1. In medium bowl, combine ground beef, onion, cracker crumbs, egg, milk, salt and pepper, mixing lightly but thoroughly.

2. Shape hamburger mixture into 4 (½ inch thick) patties.

3. Heat large nonstick skillet over medium heat until hot. Place beef patties in skillet; cook 12 to 15 minutes or until centers are no longer pink, turning once.

4. Use same skillet with pan drippings to prepare gravy mix according to package directions, drizzle over steak and serve.

Makes 4 servings

Nutrition Information

230 calories, 8 grams fat, 130 mg cholesterol, 560 mg sodium,
8 grams carbohydrate, 0 grams fiber, 31 grams protein

Exchanges: 0.5 carbohydrate, 4.5 protein, 1.5 fat

SIMPLE BEEF STROGANOFF

Ingredients

1-¼ pounds boneless sirloin steak

1 medium onion, sliced

1 tablespoon olive oil

1 (10.75 oz) can Campbell's Healthy Request Cream of Mushroom Soup

1 (14 oz) can of beef broth

½ cup water

3 cups dry egg noodles

½ cup light sour cream

Directions

1. Slice beef into very thin strips.

2. In a nonstick skillet sauté beef and onion slices in olive oil over medium heat until browned, stirring often. Remove from skillet and set aside.

3. Add soup, broth and water to skillet and bring to a boil. Stir in noodles. Cook over a low heat for 10 minutes or until noodles are tender, stirring often. Stir in sour cream.

4. Return beef to sour cream mixture and heat through, but do not boil.

Makes 6 servings

Nutrition Information

320 calories, 14 grams fat, 80 mg cholesterol, 270 mg sodium, 22 grams carbohydrate, 2 grams fiber, 26 grams protein

Exchanges: 1.5 carbohydrate, 4 protein, 3 fat

SLOW-COOKER POT ROAST

Ingredients

1 (4 lb) eye-of-round roast, trimmed

2 teaspoons salt

1 teaspoon freshly ground
black pepper

1 tablespoon canola oil

1 (1 lb) baby carrots

1 lb small new potatoes, cut in half

1 (14.5 oz) can petite diced tomatoes

1 cup chopped celery

1 cup beef broth

½ cup water or red wine

2 garlic cloves, chopped

1 teaspoon dried thyme leaves

Directions

1. Rub roast evenly with 2 teaspoons salt and 1 teaspoon pepper.

2. Brown roast on all sides in hot oil in a Dutch oven over medium-high heat (about 10 minutes). Place roast in slow cooker. Add carrots and remaining ingredients.

3. Cook, covered, on LOW 10 to 12 hours or until tender. Remove roast from slow cooker; let roast rest for 5 minutes, slice and serve with vegetables and gravy mixture.

   Makes 10 servings

Nutrition Information

290 calories, 10 grams fat, 115 mg cholesterol, 730 mg sodium,
10 grams carbohydrate, 3 grams fiber, 38 grams protein

Exchanges: 0.5 carbohydrate, 5.5 protein, 2 fat

SPICY ORANGE BEEF STIR FRY

Ingredients

1 teaspoon minced garlic

½ teaspoon crushed red pepper

1 pound boneless sirloin steak, cut into ¼-inch strips

½ teaspoon grated orange zest

¼ cup fresh orange juice

1 tablespoon cornstarch

2 tablespoons low-sodium soy sauce

1 teaspoon dark sesame oil

¾ cup (1-inch) sliced green onions

2 cups cooked brown rice

Directions

1. Combine garlic, pepper and beef tossing well; set aside.

2. Whisk together zest, juice, cornstarch and soy sauce in small bowl, set aside.

3. Heat oil in a large nonstick skillet over medium-high heat. Add beef mixture and onions; sauté 2 minutes. Add juice mixture; cook 2 minutes or until sauce thickens, stirring frequently. Serve beef over rice.

Makes 4 servings

Nutrition Information

280 calories, 7 grams fat, 40 mg cholesterol, 540 mg sodium, 28 grams carbohydrate, 2 grams fiber, 26 grams protein

Exchanges: 2 carbohydrate, 4 protein, 1 fat

TEXAS BEEF SKILLET

Ingredients

1-½ pounds 95% lean ground beef

1 can (15 oz) tomatoes
with green chilies

1 can (15 oz) black beans,
drained and rinsed

1 cup frozen corn

1 cup cooked brown rice

¼ cup water

½ teaspoon each salt,
garlic salt, and black pepper

1 teaspoon chili powder

1 cup low fat sharp cheddar cheese
shreds

Directions

1. In a large skillet, brown the ground beef; and drain well.

2. Stir in tomatoes, black beans, corn, brown rice, water and seasonings. Bring to a boil, reduce heat and simmer 2-3 minutes, until heated through.

3. Top with cheese shreds and serve.

Makes 6 servings

Nutrition information

330 calories, 8 grams fat, 85 mg cholesterol, 990 mg sodium,
23 grams carbohydrate, 5 grams fiber, 39 grams protein

Exchanges: 1.5 carbohydrate, 5.5 protein, 1.5 fat

Lemon Spinach Chicken, p. 47

Chicken

Looking for something quick and easy for dinner that is a surefire family pleaser? Chicken is the perfect choice. I love serving chicken because it is so versatile. It can be pounded flat to cook in minutes in a skillet, sliced for a stir-fry or slathered with BBQ sauce and thrown on the grill.

When counseling patients on how to eat healthy, they often assume they will be destined to a life of dry, white meat chicken. What they don't know is – I am a 'foodie' first and a dietitian second. I love delicious food, and I think life is too short to eat bad food. One of the first things I show them is a list of condiments to use to add flavor. The secret to a great chicken dish is to not overcook the chicken. Most chicken breasts will cook in about 15 - 20 minutes on the grill and about 25 to 30 minutes in a moderate oven. They are cooked through when they reach an internal temperature of 170 degrees.

I've included two recipes in this section that are hands down my children's favorites – affectionately known at our house as *Jan's Chicken* (page 46) and *Cornflake Chicken* (page 41). I discovered long ago that kids are more likely to eat when they have helped prepare the food, plus it gives you quality time together. Pour the crackers or cornflakes into a heavy-duty ziplock bag, give your child a rolling pin and let them help make dinner!

Chicken Facts...

- To skin or not to skin?
  One 4-oz chicken breast with skin contains 188 calories and 10 grams of fat while a 4-oz skinless chicken breast contains only 120 calories and 3 grams of fat. Why not add taste and save the calories by using low-fat sauces and marinades instead of leaving the skin on?
- Chicken is one of the best sources of lean protein – a 4 oz portion contains about 22 grams of protein.

Ingredients

2 (10 oz) packages frozen broccoli spears

6 boneless, skinless chicken breast halves, cooked and sliced

2 (10.75 oz) cans Campbell's Healthy Request Cream of Chicken Soup

1 cup light mayonnaise

1 teaspoon fresh lemon juice

½ teaspoon curry powder

½ cup reduced-fat cheddar cheese shreds

½ cup panko breadcrumbs

1 tablespoon butter, melted

Directions

1. Cook broccoli in boiling water until tender; drain. Arrange spears in greased 9 X 13-inch glass dish.

2. Place chicken on top of broccoli.

3. Combine soup, mayonnaise, lemon juice and curry powder; pour over chicken. Sprinkle with cheese.

4. Combine breadcrumbs and butter. Sprinkle over all. Bake at 350 degrees for 20 minutes or until bubbly.

   Makes 8 servings

Nutrition Information

330 calories, 16 grams fat, 75 mg cholesterol, 510 mg sodium, 23 grams carbohydrate, 3 grams fiber, 25 grams protein

Exchanges: 1.5 carbohydrate, 3.5 protein, 3 fat

Ingredients

2 tablespoons butter

¼ cup flour

1 (14 oz) can low-sodium chicken broth

1 cup 1% milk

2 cups cooked chicken, cubed

2 cups peas and carrots

1 hard-boiled egg, sliced thin

½ teaspoon salt

¼ teaspoon poultry seasoning

¼ teaspoon pepper

1 9-inch pie crust (refrigerated)

Directions

1. Melt butter in heavy Dutch oven; add flour; stirring until smooth. Cook 1 minute, stirring constantly. Gradually add broth and milk; cook over medium heat; stirring constantly, until thick and bubbly. Stir in remaining ingredients; except pie crust.

2. Pour chicken mixture into a deep 1-½ quart baking dish. Top with pie crust. Cut slits in crust to allow steam to escape. Bake at 400 degrees for 25 to 30 minutes or until crust is golden brown.

   Makes 4 servings

Nutrition Information

460 calories, 21 grams fat, 140 mg cholesterol, 420 mg sodium, 34 grams carbohydrate, 3 grams fiber, 31 grams protein

Exchanges: 2 carbohydrate, 4.5 protein, 4 fat

CHICKEN WITH SNOW PEAS

Ingredients

2 (4 oz) skinless boneless chicken breast halves

1 teaspoon canola oil

1 cup celery, diced

1 medium onion

1 cup fresh snow peas

½ cup canned sliced water chestnuts

½ cup fat-free chicken broth

1 tablespoon soy sauce

1 teaspoon cornstarch

1 teaspoon sugar

1-⅓ cups cooked brown rice

Directions

1. Cut chicken into thin strips; sprinkle with salt and pepper. Sauté chicken in hot oil in a large non-stick skillet until lightly browned.

2. Add celery, onion, pea pods, water chestnuts and 2 tablespoons broth; cover skillet and cook over low heat for 1-½ minutes.

3. Combine soy sauce, cornstarch, and sugar, stirring well; stir into chicken mixture.

4. Gradually add remaining broth. Cook, stirring constantly, until thickened. Serve over brown rice.

Makes 2 servings

Nutrition Information

450 calories, 7 grams fat, 85 mg cholesterol, 710 mg sodium, 56 grams carbohydrate, 8 grams fiber, 41 grams protein

Exchanges: 4 carbohydrate, 6 protein, 1.5 fat

CORNFLAKE CHICKEN

Ingredients

2 cups cornflakes

1 teaspoon salt

½ teaspoon pepper

¼ cup butter

4 (5 oz) chicken breast halves, pounded to even thickness

Directions

1. Place cornflakes, salt and pepper in plastic zip-lock bag. Crush gently with rolling pin; set aside.

2. Melt butter in microwave-safe bowl. Dip chicken into butter then place one at a time into bag with cornflake mixture. Shake to cover and place in a single layer in 8 ½ X 11-inch Pyrex dish.

3. Sprinkle remaining cornflakes from bag over chicken. Drizzle with remaining butter. Bake uncovered at 375 degrees for 30 minutes or until chicken is cooked through.

Makes 4 servings

Nutrition Information

300 calories, 15 grams fat, 110 mg cholesterol, 840 mg sodium, 12 grams carbohydrate, 0 grams fiber, 30 grams protein

Exchanges: 1 carbohydrate, 4 protein, 3 fat

EASY CHICKEN & DUMPLINGS

Ingredients

4 boneless, skinless chicken breasts

3 large carrots, peeled and sliced

1 onion, chopped

2 (14 oz) cans low-sodium chicken broth

2 cups water

½ teaspoon each salt, black pepper and parsley flakes

1 (7.5 oz) can buttermilk biscuits (not flaky)

Directions

1. Boil chicken breasts, carrots, onions, and seasonings in broth and 2 cups water for 20 minutes or until done.

2. Remove chicken and cut into bite-sized pieces and set aside.

3. With kitchen shears snip biscuits into quarters. Add one at a time to boiling broth to allow dumplings to puff up. Cover and cook without stirring for approximately 10 minutes. May add additional broth if needed.

4. Remove lid and stir dumplings into broth. Add diced chicken, simmer for 5 minutes to heat through and serve.

Makes 4 servings

Nutrition Information

300 calories, 4.5 grams fat, 70 mg cholesterol, 992 mg sodium, 47 grams carbohydrate, 2 grams fiber, 31 grams protein

Exchanges: 3 carbohydrate, 4.5 protein, 1 fat

Ingredients

4 skinless, boneless chicken breasts

1 (8 oz) package reduced-fat cream cheese

1 (10 oz) can Rotel tomatoes with green chilies

16 corn tortillas

2 (14 oz) cans green enchilada sauce

½ cup queso fresco, crumbled

Directions

1. Place chicken breasts in glass baking dish and bake at 350 degrees for 30 minutes; dice and set aside.

2. In large skillet, combine cream cheese and tomatoes w/green chilies. Cook over low heat until cream cheese is melted. Add diced chicken and set aside.

3. Warm tortillas; divide chicken mixture between the tortillas. Roll and place in greased 9 X 13-inch Pyrex baking dish.

4. Cover with enchilada sauce. Bake at 400 degrees for 20 minutes or until hot and bubbly. Remove from oven, sprinkle with queso fresco and serve.

Makes 8 servings

Nutrition Information

260 calories, 11 grams fat, 55 mg cholesterol, 750 mg sodium, 19 grams carbohydrate, 2 grams fiber, 20 grams protein

Exchanges: 1 carbohydrate, 3 protein, 2 fat

HONEY-PECAN CHICKEN

Ingredients

2 tablespoons lite soy sauce

2 tablespoons honey

2 cups wheat cereal squares, crushed

⅓ cup finely chopped pecans

1 teaspoon salt

1 teaspoon pepper

6 skinless, boneless chicken breast halves

Vegetable cooking spray

Directions

1. Stir together soy sauce and honey; set mixture aside.
2. Combine cereal crumbs, pecans, salt and pepper.
3. Dip both sides of chicken breast in soy sauce mixture; dredge in crumb mixture to coat.
4. Arrange chicken breasts on an aluminum-foil lined baking sheet coated with cooking spray. Sprinkle remaining crumb mixture on top of chicken.
5. Bake at 425 degrees for 20 to 25 minutes.

   Makes 6 servings

Nutrition Information

270 calories, 8 grams fat, 85 mg cholesterol, 840 mg sodium, 15 grams carbohydrate, 2 grams fiber, 33 grams protein

Exchanges: 1 carbohydrate, 5 protein, 1.5 fat

JALAPENO ORANGE CHICKEN

Ingredients

1 cup chopped onion

½ cup chopped green bell pepper

1 to 2 jalapeno peppers, finely chopped

1 to 2 cloves of garlic, minced

2 tablespoons butter

6 skinless, boneless chicken breasts

¼ cup flour

¼ teaspoon each salt and pepper

½ cup fresh orange juice

½ cup chicken broth

3 cups cooked brown rice

Directions

1. In large skillet, sauté onion, bell pepper, jalapenos and garlic in butter until tender. Remove from skillet; set aside.

2. In medium bowl, combine flour, salt and pepper. Dip chicken breasts into flour mixture. Heat same skillet and add chicken – browning on both sides.

3. When browned, add orange juice, chicken broth and reserved vegetables. Cover and simmer for 20 minutes or until chicken is cooked through. Serve over hot steamed brown rice.

Makes 6 servings

Nutrition Information

390 calories, 8 grams fat, 85 mg cholesterol, 360 mg sodium, 32 grams carbohydrate, 3 grams fiber, 31 grams protein

Exchanges: 2 carbohydrate, 4.5 protein, 1.5 fat

JAN'S CHICKEN

Ingredients

2 sleeves reduced-fat Ritz crackers, crushed

4 tablespoons butter

4 skinless, boneless chicken breast halves, cooked

1 (16 oz) carton reduced-fat sour cream

2 (10.75 oz) cans Campbell's Healthy Request Cream of Chicken Soup

Directions

1. Combine cracker crumbs with butter (reserve 1 cup for topping). Press remaining crumbs into 9 X 13-inch Pyrex dish and set aside.

2. Cut cooked chicken breast into bite-sized pieces and set aside.

3. Mix together sour cream and soup; stir in chicken.

4. Gently spread mixture over crumb crust and sprinkle reserved crumbs on top. Bake at 350 degrees for 20 minutes or until bubbly.

Makes 8 servings

Nutrition Information

370 calories, 19 grams fat, 90 mg cholesterol, 360 mg sodium, 29 grams carbohydrate, 1 gram fiber, 21 grams protein

Exchanges: 2 carbohydrate, 3 protein, 4 fat

Ingredients

4 (5 oz) skinless, boneless chicken breast halves

½ cup all-purpose flour

¾ teaspoon salt

½ teaspoon freshly ground pepper

1-½ tablespoons each, butter & olive oil

2 garlic cloves, minced

1 cup low-sodium chicken broth

½ cup dry white wine

2 tablespoons lemon juice

4 slices tomato

¼ cup reduced-fat Swiss cheese shreds

4 cups fresh baby spinach

Directions

1. Place chicken breasts between double layer of plastic wrap. Pound, with meat mallet, to ¼-inch thickness.

2. Combine flour, salt and pepper in a shallow dish; dredge chicken in mixture.

3. Heat butter and olive oil in a large skillet; add chicken and cook 3 minutes on each side or until golden. Remove chicken from skillet, reserving drippings in pan.

4. Add garlic to hot skillet and brown for 1 minute. Stir in broth, wine, and lemon juice. Loosening browned particles in skillet; bring to a boil. Return chicken to skillet; reduce heat; top chicken breast with tomato slice and 1 tablespoon of Swiss cheese. Cover and simmer for 5 minutes.

5. Place 1 cup spinach on each plate; spoon chicken and sauce over spinach and serve. (Spinach will wilt when covered with hot chicken.)

Makes 4 servings

Nutrition Information

340 calories, 13 grams fat, 95 mg cholesterol, 740 mg sodium, 17 grams carbohydrate, 2 grams fiber, 34 grams protein

Exchanges: 1 carbohydrate, 5 protein, 2.5 fat

MEXICAN SPAGHETTI

Ingredients

1 (8 oz) package whole wheat spaghetti

1 (14 oz) can chicken broth

1 onion, chopped

1 tablespoon butter

1 (10 oz) can Rotel tomatoes with green chilies

½ pound Velveeta Light, cubed

3 cups cooked chicken, cubed

Directions

1. Cook spaghetti in chicken broth, plus 2 cans water, drain and set aside.

2. Place onions and butter in large microwave-safe bowl, cook for 1 minute, stopping to stir at 30 seconds.

3. Add Rotel tomatoes and microwave for 1 minute. Add cheese and microwave for 2 minutes or until cheese is melted. Stir in chicken and spaghetti.

4. Transfer spaghetti mixture to 9 X 13-inch Pyrex baking dish coated with cooking spray.

5. Bake at 350 degrees for 20 minutes, or until bubbly.

   Makes 8 servings

Nutrition Information

280 calories, 7 grams fat, 60 mg cholesterol, 670 mg sodium, 27 grams carbohydrate, 4 grams fiber, 27 grams protein

Exchanges: 2 carbohydrate, 4 protein, 1 fat

SZECHUAN CHICKEN WITH ANGEL HAIR PASTA

Ingredients

8 ounces angel hair pasta

1 tablespoon dark sesame oil

2 tablespoons chili garlic sauce, divided

4 (5 oz) skinless, boneless chicken breasts

1-½ pounds fresh broccoli florets*

1 red or yellow bell pepper, cut into ½-inch strips

6 green onions, sliced

2 teaspoons minced garlic

¼ cup light soy sauce

¼ cup low-sodium chicken broth

½ tablespoon minced fresh ginger

*may purchase in a bag in produce section

Directions

1. Cook pasta according to package directions, keep warm.

2. Combine oil and 1 tablespoon chile garlic sauce in a skillet; add chicken, and cook 5 minutes on each side or until done. Remove chicken from pan, and cut into strips.

3. Add vegetables, minced garlic, remaining 1 tablespoon chile garlic sauce, soy sauce, chicken broth and minced ginger to skillet; cook until vegetables are crisp-tender. Add chicken strips; cook until thoroughly heated. Add pasta, toss and serve.

Makes 6 servings

Nutrition Information

330 calories, 7 grams fat, 95 mg cholesterol, 840 mg sodium, 32 grams carbohydrate, 5 grams fiber, 36 grams protein

Exchanges: 2 carbohydrate, 5 protein, 1 fat

Slow Cooker Root Beer Pulled Pork, p. 57

Pork

Tired of chicken? Did you know pork is called 'the other white meat' for good reason? It is quick to fix, versatile and comparable in calories and fat to skinless, boneless chicken breast.

One of my favorite meals is pork tenderloin on the grill. Simply marinate, grill, slice and serve. What could be easier? I've included my recipe for *Molasses Grilled Pork Tenderloin* (page 54) for you to try. It is delicious served with fresh grilled corn on the cob and *Sunflower Spinach Salad* (page 13).

There is nothing better than coming home after a busy day to dinner ready in the slow cooker! The *Pork Chalupas* (page 55) and the *Slow Cooker Root Beer Pulled Pork* (page 57) are definite crowd pleasers! Take a few minutes to prepare them in the morning before you leave and when you walk in the door, exhausted from the day, the aroma that greets you is amazing! These recipes make enough to serve your family AND to enjoy as leftovers for lunch or busy evenings later in the week.

Did you know...

- One 4-oz serving of pork tenderloin has 130 calories, 24 grams of protein, and 5 grams of fat.
- When trimmed, pork contains very little saturated fat and is an excellent source of iron, zinc, some B vitamins, selenium and phosphorus.
- According to the National Pork Board, pork is done when a meat thermometer registers 145 degrees when inserted into the thickest part of the meat.

GRILLED JALAPENO-BASIL PORK CHOPS

Ingredients

1 cup jalapeno pepper jelly

½ cup dry white wine

¼ cup chopped fresh basil leaves

4 (1-inch thick) bone-in pork chops

½ teaspoon each salt and fresh ground black pepper

Directions

1. In small saucepan, stir together jelly and wine. Heat over low heat until jelly is melted. Remove from heat, stir in basil and let mixture cool completely.

2. Pour ¾ cup pepper jelly mixture into a large zip-lock plastic bag, reserving remaining mixture; add pork chops, turning to coat. Seal and place in refrigerator to marinate.

3. Remove chops from marinade, discarding marinade. Sprinkle evenly with salt and pepper.

4. Grill, covered with grill lid, over medium-high heat 5 to 8 minutes on each side or until a meat thermometer inserted into thickest portion registers 145 degrees. Serve with remaining pepper jelly mixture.

   Makes 4 servings (1 pork chop + 1 tablespoon glaze)

Nutrition Information

250 calories, 11 grams fat, 60 mg cholesterol, 350 mg sodium, 14 grams carbohydrate, 0 grams fiber, 21 grams protein

Exchanges: 1 carbohydrate, 3 protein, 2 fat

Dinner in a flash – ready in less than 30 minutes & tastes like you were in the kitchen all day!! Just cooking for two? This recipe is easy to adjust – cut all ingredients in half and you have just enough for two!

Ingredients

6 ounces whole wheat angel hair pasta

2 slices center cut bacon, cut into ½-inch pieces

½ cup onion, chopped

1 cup fresh sliced mushrooms

1 cup sliced celery

1 medium zucchini, sliced

4 oz reduced-fat cream cheese

1-¼ cup 1% milk

1 cup reduced-fat Swiss cheese shreds

¼ cup Parmesan cheese shreds

1 cup 97% lean ham, cut into cubes

½ teaspoon each salt and pepper

Directions

1. Prepare pasta as directed on package; set aside.
2. Meanwhile, sauté bacon in large non-stick skillet. Add onion, mushrooms, celery and zucchini and cook for 5 minutes over medium heat. Add cubed cream cheese and stir constantly over low heat. Add milk, cheeses, ham, salt and pepper.
3. Cook through until all cheese is melted. Stir in pasta and serve. (May add additional milk if mixture is too thick.)

Makes 4 servings

Nutrition Information

400 calories, 13 grams fat, 55 mg cholesterol, 1080 mg sodium, 43 grams carbohydrate, 7 grams fiber, 31 grams protein

Exchanges: 3 carbohydrate, 4.5 protein, 2.5 fat

MOLASSES-GRILLED PORK TENDERLOIN

Ingredients

½ cup molasses

2 tablespoons Dijon mustard

1 tablespoon apple cider vinegar

4 (¾ pound) pork tenderloins

Directions

1. Combine molasses, Dijon mustard, and vinegar; brush over tenderloins. Cover and marinate in refrigerator for 8 hours.

2. Cook, covered with grill lid, over medium heat for about 20-30 minutes, turning once. Pork is done when meat thermometer inserted in thickest portion registers 145 degrees.

   Makes 10 servings

Nutrition Information

180 calories, 5 grams fat, 75 mg cholesterol, 130 mg sodium, 7 grams carbohydrate, 0 grams fiber, 27 grams protein

Exchanges: 0.5 carbohydrate, 4 protein, 1 fat

Ingredients

2 pounds pork roast or pork tenderloin

1 pound dried pinto beans, uncooked

2 cloves garlic

2 tablespoons chili powder

1 tablespoon cumin

1 teaspoon Tabasco sauce

¼ cup salsa

1 large onion, chopped

2-½ cups canned tomatoes

½ teaspoon each salt and pepper

Optional Toppings
Bite sized tortilla chips, shredded lettuce, grated cheese, chopped tomatoes, sliced avocado, and salsa for garnish.

Directions

1. Place roast in crock pot and cover with water.
2. Add washed pinto beans and remaining ingredients.
3. Cover and cook at least 8 hours, stirring occasionally.
4. Adjust or correct any seasonings during last 2 hours of cooking.
5. Serve over tortilla chips, garnished with lettuce, cheese, tomato, avocado and salsa, as desired.

   Makes 8 servings

Nutrition Information

360 calories, 4.5 grams fat, 65 mg cholesterol, 420 mg sodium, 41 grams carbohydrate, 10 grams fiber, 36 grams protein

Exchanges: 2.5 carbohydrate, 5 proteins, 1 fat

Ingredients

4 (5 oz) center cut pork chops, trimmed of all fat

1 tablespoon olive oil

1 cup apple, chopped

1 cup celery, chopped

1 cup onion, chopped

1 (14 oz) can low-sodium chicken broth

1 (6 oz) box instant wild rice mix

Directions

1. In large skillet, brown pork chops in olive oil for 2 to 3 minutes on each side. Remove from skillet and set aside.

2. In same skillet, sauté apples, celery and onions in pan drippings for about 5 minutes or until just tender.

3. Add chicken broth and water to make 2 cups of liquid. Stir in rice and seasoning packet. Place pork chops on top and cook over low heat for 5 minutes.

Makes 4 servings

Nutrition Information

440 calories, 12 grams fat, 90 mg cholesterol, 370 mg sodium, 43 grams carbohydrate, 4 grams fiber, 36 grams protein

Exchanges: 3 carbohydrate, 5 protein, 2 fat

SLOW COOKER ROOT BEER PULLED PORK

Great served with Coleslaw!

Ingredients

1 (3-½ pound) lean pork roast

1 teaspoon BBQ rub

1 (12 oz) bottle root beer (not diet)

1 (18 oz) bottle of your favorite barbecue sauce

12 whole wheat hamburger buns

Directions

1. Rub pork with 1 teaspoon barbecue rub and place in slow cooker; pour root beer over the meat.

2. Cover and cook on low until tender and pork shreds easily, about 8 hours.

3. Remove pork from slow cooker and shred. Pour drippings into container and set aside.

4. Place shredded pork back into slow cooker, add barbecue sauce and desired amount of drippings to get moist consistency; cook on low until heated through.

   Makes 12 (or more) servings

Nutrition Information

370 calories, 13 grams fat, 85 mg cholesterol, 760 mg sodium, 35 grams carbohydrate, 3 grams fiber, 29 grams protein

Exchanges: 2 carbohydrate, 4 protein, 2.5 fat

SMOTHERED PORK CHOPS

Ingredients

6 (5 oz) thick center cut pork chops

½ cup flour

1 teaspoon salt

½ teaspoon pepper

2 tablespoons canola oil

Directions

1. On waxed paper, combine flour, salt and pepper. Coat pork chops lightly with flour mixture.

2. In skillet, over medium-high heat, in hot oil, brown pork chops on both sides.

3. Place in Pyrex dish; add 1 cup water to pan drippings and pour over pork chops.

4. Cover with foil and bake at 325 degree for 45 minutes to 1 hour depending on thickness of chops.

   Makes 6 servings

Nutrition Information

270 calories, 13 grams fat, 80 mg cholesterol, 450 mg sodium, 7 grams carbohydrate, 0 grams fiber, 33 grams protein

Exchanges: 0.5 carbohydrate, 5 protein, 2.5 fat

Ingredients

1 tablespoon canola oil

4 (4 oz) boneless center cut pork chops

1 onion, thinly sliced

¼ teaspoon each caraway seeds, paprika, dried whole dill weed

Dash of garlic powder

¼ teaspoon salt

⅔ cup reduced-fat sour cream

Directions

1. Heat oil in heavy skillet over medium heat. Brown pork chops on both sides. Remove from skillet; set aside.

2. Add onion to skillet and sauté for 2 minutes. Add seasonings and 1 cup water; bring to boil. Return pork chops to skillet, cover, reduce heat and simmer 20 minutes, adding more water as needed to prevent sticking. Remove pork chops from skillet onto serving platter.

3. Stir sour cream into drippings, heat through, but do not boil. Ladle over pork chops and serve.

Makes 4 servings

Nutrition Information

270 calories, 15 grams fat, 85 mg cholesterol, 220 mg sodium, 6 grams carbohydrate, 1 gram fiber, 26 grams protein

Exchanges: 0.5 carbohydrate, 4 protein, 3 fat

Pan Roasted Salmon with Tomato Citrus Salsa, p. 65

Seafood

I often hear clients say, "I don't have the time or money to cook healthy", and I immediately think of fish! Did you know tilapia is a very inexpensive, mild-flavored white fish that can be cooked and ready to put on the table in 10 minutes! It is much quicker and cheaper than picking up fast food and I've included a delicious recipe for you - *Crispy Baked Tilapia* (page 63) - that your entire family will love!

Salmon is a fabulous source of heart healthy omega-3's. I've included one of my favorites for the grill, *Salmon with Brown Sugar Mustard Glaze* (page 66), it is quick-to-fix and amazing to eat!

And then there is the ultimate fast food – shrimp! Check out the recipe for *Cajun Shrimp Pasta* (page 62) – a crowd-pleaser that is ready to eat in less than 20 minutes!

Did you know...

- 2010 U.S. Dietary Guidelines recommend eating fish at least two times a week for cardiac and brain benefit.
- A 4-oz serving of tilapia has only 93 calories and 21 grams of protein.

CAJUN SHRIMP PASTA

Ingredients

6 ounces whole wheat angel hair pasta

¼ cup butter

3 cloves garlic minced

¼ cup chopped green onion

1-½ teaspoons Tony Chachere's Spicy Creole Seasoning, or to taste

1 teaspoon cracked fresh black pepper

1 cup white wine

1 cup diced plum tomatoes

1 pound medium shrimp, peeled and deveined

1 cup baby spinach

Directions

1. Bring a large pot of lightly salted water to a boil. Add pasta, cook for 5 minutes, until almost al dente; drain.

2. Melt butter in a medium skillet over medium heat. Stir in garlic and green onion. Season with Cajun seasoning and pepper, and cook about 2 minutes. Stir in wine, tomatoes and shrimp.

3. Continue to cook and stir until shrimp are opaque. Mix in pasta and spinach, cover and simmer for 3 to 5 minutes, until pasta is al dente and spinach is wilted.

Makes 6 servings

Nutrition Information

260 calories, 6 grams fat, 125 mg cholesterol, 340 mg sodium, 26 grams carbohydrate, 4 grams fiber, 20 grams protein

Exchanges: 1.5 carbohydrate, 3 protein, 1 fat

CRISPY BAKED TILAPIA

Ingredients

1 cup panko breadcrumbs

2 tablespoons chopped fresh parsley

2 teaspoons grated lemon zest

1 teaspoon minced garlic

4 (5 oz.) tilapia fillets

½ teaspoon salt

2 tablespoons butter, melted

Directions

1. Combine first 4 ingredients in a small bowl.

2. Place fillets in a lightly greased baking dish; sprinkle evenly with salt. Spoon breadcrumb mixture evenly onto fillets, pressing down gently. Drizzle evenly with melted butter.

3. Bake at 450 degrees for 8 to 10 minutes or until breadcrumbs are golden and fish flakes with a fork.

Makes 4 servings

Nutrition Information

270 calories, 8 grams fat, 70 mg cholesterol, 430 mg sodium, 25 grams carbohydrate, 0 grams fiber, 24 grams protein

Exchanges: 1.5 carbohydrate, 3.5 protein, 1.5 fat

ONE-POT SHRIMP PAELLA

Ingredients

1 tablespoon olive oil

1-½ cups diced lean ham

1 cup chopped onion

1 cup chopped red bell pepper

1 pound large shrimp, peeled and deveined

1-¼ cups arborio rice

3-¼ cups (or more) low-sodium chicken broth, divided

¼ teaspoon saffron threads, crumbled (if desired)

¼ teaspoon hot Spanish paprika or hot Hungarian paprika

½ teaspoon salt

¼ teaspoon pepper

¼ cup pimiento-stuffed olives, halved

Directions

1. Heat oil in heavy large skillet over medium-high heat.

2. Add ham, onions, bell pepper and sauté 5 minutes. Add shrimp and sauté an additional 3 to 4 minutes; remove from skillet and set aside. In same skillet, add rice, broth, saffron, paprika, salt and pepper.

3. Reduce heat to low, cover, and simmer until rice is almost tender, about 15 minutes.

4. Stir shrimp mixture into rice, top with olives, and drizzle with ¼ cup (or more) broth to moisten.

5. Cover and cook over low heat until heated through, about 3 to 5 minutes. Adjust seasoning to taste with more salt and pepper, if needed.

Makes 6 servings

Nutrition Information

340 calories, 8 grams fat, 120 mg cholesterol, 590 mg sodium, 38 grams carbohydrate, 3 grams fiber, 28 grams protein

Exchanges: 2.5 carbohydrate, 4 protein, 1.5 fat

PAN ROASTED SALMON WITH TOMATO-CITRUS SALSA

Ingredients

3 large oranges, sectioned and divided

4 (6 oz) skinless salmon fillets

1 tablespoon olive oil

½ cup thinly sliced red onion

1-½ cups diced Roma tomatoes

2 tablespoons capers

1 teaspoon salt, divided

½ teaspoon black pepper, divided

Directions

1. In medium bowl, zest ½ teaspoon orange rind. Add ¼ cup fresh orange juice from 1 orange. Section remaining 2 oranges over bowl; set aside.

2. Season salmon fillets with ½ teaspoon salt and ¼ teaspoon black pepper.

3. Place olive oil in large, oven proof skillet over medium-high heat. Add salmon, top side down and cook for 5 minutes. Remove fish from pan and set aside.

4. Add onions and cook for 3 minutes.

5. Pour orange juice from bowl into skillet – holding orange sections to be added later.

6. Add orange sections, tomatoes, capers, ½ teaspoon salt and ¼ teaspoon black pepper; cook for 2 minutes stirring occasionally.

7. Add salmon, browned side up, on top of tomato mixture. Place skillet in oven and bake at 400 degrees for 5 minutes or to desired degree of doneness.

Makes 4 servings

Nutrition Information

320 calories, 11 grams fat, 80 mg cholesterol, 880 mg sodium, 18 grams carbohydrate, 4 grams fiber, 38 grams protein

Exchanges: 1 carbohydrate, 5.5 protein, 2 fat

Ingredients

1 tablespoon brown sugar

1 teaspoon honey

2 tablespoons butter

2 tablespoons Dijon mustard

1 tablespoon lite soy sauce

1 tablespoon olive oil

2 teaspoons grated fresh ginger

6 (5 oz) salmon fillets

Directions

1. Preheat grill.

2. In small saucepan, combine brown sugar, honey, and butter; heat just until melted. Remove from heat and whisk in mustard, soy sauce, olive oil and ginger; set aside.

3. Place salmon, top side down, on hot grill. Cook 3 to 4 minutes, or until lightly brown. Turn fillets and brush with brown sugar mustard glaze. Cook about 5 minutes or to desired degree of doneness.

Makes 6 servings

Nutrition Information

240 calories, 12 grams fat, 70 mg cholesterol, 410 mg sodium, 6 grams carbohydrates, 0 grams fiber, 27 grams protein

Exchanges: 0.5 carbohydrate, 4 protein, 2 fat

Here's a delicious, nutritious meal you can make in minutes!

Ingredients

3 tablespoons low-sodium soy sauce

1 tablespoon orange juice

1 teaspoon sugar

1 tablespoon minced fresh ginger

2 tablespoons canola oil

1 pound large shrimp, peeled and deveined

2 tablespoons sesame seeds

½ red bell pepper, sliced

½ cup sliced green onions

2 cups steamed brown rice

Directions

1. In small bowl, combine soy sauce, orange juice, sugar and ginger.
2. Heat wok or large skillet on high heat; add oil. Add shrimp and sesame seeds; reduce heat to medium-high and stir-fry for 1 minute. Add soy mixture, peppers and green onions; stir-fry for 2 minutes or until shrimp are done. Serve over rice.

   Makes 4 servings

Nutrition Information

340 calories, 12 grams fat, 170 mg cholesterol, 860 mg sodium, 29 grams carbohydrate, 3 grams fiber, 27 grams protein

Exchanges: 2 carbohydrate, 4 protein, 2 fat

SHRIMP BOIL HOBO DINNERS

Ingredients

24 large shrimp, peeled and deveined

4 oz. reduced fat kielbasa-style sausage, sliced ½ inch thick

2 large ears of corn, shucked and cut into 4 rounds

4 thyme sprigs

1-½ tablespoons unsalted butter, cut into 4 pieces

1 teaspoon Old Bay seasoning

1 teaspoon spicy Creole seasoning

½ teaspoon fresh cracked black pepper

¼ cup dry white wine

¼ cup water

Directions

1. Light grill. Lay four 24-by-18-inch sheets of heavy-duty foil on a work surface. Arrange shrimp, kielbasa, corn, thyme and butter in center of foil; season evenly with Old Bay, spicy Creole seasoning, and black pepper. Into each packet, pour 1 tablespoon each of wine and water. Bring edges of foil up over shrimp mixture and seal tightly.

2. Grill packets over moderate heat. Shake packets after 5 minutes, cook additional 10 minutes. Cut open each packet, pour contents into bowls and serve.

    Makes 4 servings

Nutrition Information

270 calories, 12 grams fat, 90 mg cholesterol, 640 mg sodium, 17 grams carbohydrate, 4 grams fiber, 21 grams protein

Exchanges: 1 carbohydrate, 3 protein, 2 fat

SPICY LEMON TILAPIA

Ingredients

1 lemon, zested

1 tablespoon toasted sesame seeds

½ teaspoon each
onion salt and pepper

¼ teaspoon each paprika and red
pepper flakes

4 (6 oz) tilapia fillets

1 teaspoon canola oil

Fresh lemon wedges

Directions

1. In small bowl, combine lemon zest, sesame seeds, onion salt, and spices. Rub spice mixture onto both sides of fish fillets.

2. Heat oil in large non-stick skillet sprayed with cooking spray.

3. Sear fish over medium-high heat for 3 minutes on each side until fish is opaque and flakes easily with a fork

4. Serve with lemon wedges.

   Makes 4 servings

Nutrition Information

170 calories, 4.5 grams fat, 70 mg cholesterol, 160 mg sodium,
2 grams carbohydrate, 29 grams protein

Exchanges: 0 carbohydrate, 4 protein, 1 fat

Vegetable Quesadillas, p. 78

Vegetarian

The 2010 USDA guidelines recommend that we fill half our plates with fruits and vegetables. They are an excellent source of vitamins, minerals, antioxidants and fiber – all very important things our bodies know how to use to build the healthiest body!

If you choose to eat strictly vegetarian, it is important that you pay special attention to getting enough protein in your diet. I have many moms who bring their teenage vegetarians to me to help guide them to get protein from something besides pizza and macaroni and cheese. It is very common for kids to go off to college, decide to experiment with being vegetarian, and end up gaining 15 pounds. As healthy vegetarians know, this is not a true vegetarian diet (where are the veggies?)! A vegetarian diet can be very healthy and delicious, but it takes some practice to get in enough lean protein. Some protein rich sources can include eggs, cheese, beans, lentils and legumes, quinoa and other whole grains, tofu and other soy products, Greek yogurt and other high protein dairy, nuts and seeds. Just be aware, many vegetarian protein sources are higher in fat calories than lean meat sources of protein, so watch packing on extra pounds!

Two of my favorite vegetarian dishes are spicy *Huevos Rancheros* (page 73) and *Spinach Lasagna* (page 76) – a deliciously rich layering of spinach, cheeses and tomato sauce – included here just for you!

Ingredients

1 (15 oz) can tomatoes
with green chilies

1 (15 oz) can black beans,
drained and rinsed

1 (15 oz) can corn, drained and rinsed

1 cup instant whole grain
brown rice, uncooked

2 cups water

½ teaspoon garlic salt

½ teaspoon black pepper

½ teaspoon chili powder

1 cup reduced-fat cheddar cheese
shreds

Directions

1. In large skillet, combine tomatoes, black beans, corn, brown rice, water and seasonings.

2. Bring to a boil, reduce heat and simmer 15 minutes, stirring occasionally.

3. Top with cheese shreds and serve.

   Makes 4 servings

Nutrition Information

310 calories, 3 grams fat, 5 mg cholesterol, 1480 mg sodium,
56 grams carbohydrate, 10 grams fiber, 16 grams protein

Exchanges: 4 carbohydrate, 2 protein, 0.5 fat

Having guests for brunch - this is quick to fix and delicious!

Ingredients

1 cup chopped onion

1 teaspoon minced garlic

1 tablespoons olive oil

1 (16 oz) can diced tomatoes with green pepper and onion

1 (10 oz) can Rotel tomatoes

½ teaspoon oregano

½ teaspoon cumin

¼ teaspoon salt

¼ teaspoon pepper

6 eggs

½ cup low-fat sharp cheddar cheese, shredded

6 corn tortillas, warmed

Directions

1. Sauté onion and garlic in olive oil.

2. Add next 6 ingredients and cook over low heat for 5 minutes and pour sauce into a 9x13-inch baking dish. Make 6 indentations in the sauce and gently break an egg into each.

3. Bake at 350 degrees for 15 minutes or until eggs set. Sprinkle with cheese and cook an additional 1 minute. Place each egg on a corn tortilla, cover with sauce and serve immediately.

   Makes 6 servings

Nutrition Information

200 calories, 9 grams fat, 215 mg cholesterol, 750 mg sodium, 20 grams carbohydrate, 3 grams fiber, 11 grams protein

Exchanges: 1.5 carbohydrate, 1.5 protein, 2 fat

PENNE PASTA WITH ASPARAGUS & TOASTED PECANS

Ingredients

1 (8 oz) package whole wheat penne pasta

1 pound fresh asparagus

1 tablespoon olive oil

1 red bell pepper, seeded and chopped

1 tablespoon garlic, minced

1 cup low-sodium chicken broth

1 teaspoon salt

½ teaspoon black pepper

3 tablespoons chopped fresh basil

½ cup shredded Parmesan cheese, divided

2 tablespoons butter

½ cup pecan halves, toasted and divided

Directions

1. Prepare pasta according to package directions; drain and keep warm.

2. Snap off tough ends of asparagus and discard. Cut spears into 2-inch bite-sized pieces.

3. Sauté asparagus in hot oil in a large skillet over medium heat for 3 minutes. Stir in red bell pepper and garlic; cook, stirring occasionally for 2 minutes. Add chicken broth and bring to boil. Reduce heat and simmer for 2 minutes or until asparagus is crisp-tender. Stir in salt and pepper.

4. Toss together pasta, asparagus mixture, basil, ¼ cup cheese, butter and ¼ cup pecans. Place in serving bowl. Sprinkle evenly with remaining ¼ cup cheese and ¼ cup pecans, and serve.

Makes 6 servings

Nutrition Information

390 calories, 17 grams fat, 20 mg cholesterol, 640 mg sodium, 49 grams carbohydrate, 8 grams fiber, 13 grams protein

Exchanges: 3 carbohydrate, 2 protein, 3 fat

Ingredients

1 (8 oz) package whole wheat penne pasta, uncooked

Cooking spray

¾ cup chopped sweet red pepper

¼ cup chopped onion

1 garlic clove, minced

* May add soy sausage crumbles, if desired

1 (14.5 oz) can diced tomatoes

2 tablespoons fresh basil, chopped

¼ teaspoon each salt and pepper

1 tablespoon flour

¼ cup evaporated skim milk

Directions

1. Cook pasta according to package directions; set aside.

2. Coat a large non-stick skillet with cooking spray; place over medium-high heat until hot. Add next 3 ingredients. Sauté until vegetables are tender.

3. Add tomatoes, basil, salt and pepper. Bring mixture to a boil. Cover, reduce heat, and simmer for 10 minutes.

4. Whisk together flour and milk; stir well. Add flour mixture to tomato mixture and cook over medium heat, stirring constantly, until slightly thickened.

5. Add pasta, stirring well. Cook over medium heat 2 to 3 minutes or until thoroughly heated. Transfer mixture to a serving bowl.

Makes 4 servings

Nutrition Information

270 calories, 2 grams fat, 0 mg cholesterol 420 mg sodium, 53 grams carbohydrate, 7 grams fiber, 10 grams protein

Exchanges: 3.5 carbohydrate, 1.5 protein, 0 fat

SPINACH LASAGNA

Ingredients

1 (32 oz) jar spaghetti sauce

1-¼ cups water

½ cup dry red wine

1 (15 oz) low-fat ricotta cheese

1 (10 oz) package frozen spinach, thawed and drained

1 egg, slightly beaten

¼ teaspoon salt

1 (9 oz) box no-boil lasagna noodles

2 cups reduced-fat Mozzarella cheese shreds

¾ cup Parmesan cheese shreds

Directions

1. In large sauce pan, combine spaghetti sauce, water, and wine. Bring to a boil; reduce heat to low and simmer for 10 minutes.

2. In medium bowl, mix ricotta cheese, spinach, egg, and salt; set aside.

3. In 9 X 13-inch Pyrex dish, spread 2 cups of spaghetti sauce mixture. Cover with single layer of noodles. Spread with one-half the ricotta cheese mixture. Sprinkle with ½ of the mozzarella and Parmesan cheese. Repeat layers, ending with cheese.

4. Cover and bake at 350 degrees for 45 minutes. Remove cover and continue baking an additional 10 minutes. Remove from oven and let sit for 15 minutes before serving.

Makes 12 servings

Nutrition Information

290 calories, 11 grams fat, 45 mg cholesterol, 440 mg sodium, 32 grams carbohydrate, 4 grams fiber, 18 grams protein

Exchanges: 2 carbohydrate, 2.5 protein, 2 fat

Ingredients

1 tablespoon olive oil

1 cup potato, diced

¼ cup onion, diced

1 cup zucchini, diced

1 cup mushrooms, sliced

1 cup tomatoes, diced

1 cup fresh spinach, coarsely chopped

2 tablespoons diced jalapenos

6 eggs, slightly beaten

2 cups low-fat Swiss cheese shreds

¼ cup 1% milk

½ teaspoon salt

¼ teaspoon black pepper

Directions

1. In large oven-proof skillet, heat olive oil over medium high heat. Sauté potato, onion, zucchini and mushrooms for 5 minutes, stirring often. Add tomatoes, spinach and diced jalapenos and cook an additional 2 minutes. Remove from heat and set aside.

2. In medium bowl, whisk together eggs, cheese, milk and seasonings. Pour egg mixture over vegetables in skillet. Use fork to help incorporate egg mixture into vegetable mixture.

3. Bake at 350 degrees for 20 minutes or until frittata is set in center.

   Makes 4 servings

Nutrition Information

290 calories, 13 grams fat, 345 mg cholesterol, 1330 mg sodium, 17 grams carbohydrate, 3 grams fiber, 26 grams protein

Exchanges: 1 carbohydrate, 4 protein, 2.5 fat

VEGETABLE QUESADILLAS

These are magically delicious – the secret is in the Tabasco sauce!

Ingredients

2 cups yellow squash, thinly sliced

1 cup sliced fresh mushrooms

1 small onion, sliced

1 cup green and red bell pepper slices

1 teaspoon salt

½ teaspoon pepper

1 teaspoon Tabasco sauce

2 cups reduced-fat colby Jack cheese shreds

4 whole wheat tortillas

Salsa, optional

Directions

1. Sauté squash, mushrooms, onion and peppers with seasonings in a large skillet, sprayed thoroughly with cooking spray, until vegetables are crisp-tender; remove from skillet.

2. Place ½ cup cheese on half of each tortilla; top evenly with vegetable mixture and another ¼ cup cheese. Fold tortilla over filling. Repeat with each tortilla.

3. Wipe skillet clean, re-spray with cooking spray, cook quesadillas over medium heat 3 to 5 minutes on each side or until lightly browned. Serve immediately with your favorite salsa.

   Makes 4 servings

Nutrition Information

200 calories, 4.5 grams fat, 10 mg cholesterol, 645 mg sodium, 27 grams carbohydrates, 3 grams fiber, 18 grams protein

Exchanges: 2 carbohydrate, 2.5 protein, 1 fat

Ingredients

1 tablespoon olive oil

1 small onion, chopped

2 cups zucchini, thinly sliced

1 cup chopped green pepper

½ teaspoon dried whole oregano

½ teaspoon garlic salt

½ teaspoon each salt and pepper

2-½ cups chopped tomatoes

1 (16 oz) can kidney beans, drained and rinsed

3 cups cooked brown rice

½ cup reduced-fat pepper jack colby cheese shreds

Directions

1. Heat oil in a large skillet, over medium-high heat. Add onion, zucchini, green pepper, oregano, garlic salt, salt and pepper and sauté for 5 minutes or until tender.

2. Add tomatoes and beans; cover and heat thoroughly.

3. Spoon vegetable mixture over hot rice; sprinkle with cheese.

Makes 4 servings

Nutrition Information

210 calories, 8 grams fat, 10 mg cholesterol, 770 mg sodium, 28 grams carbohydrate, 8 grams fiber, 12 grams protein

Exchanges: 2 carbohydrate, 2 protein, 1.5 fat

Peanut Chicken Pitas, p. 88

Sandwiches

Many of us have discovered that taking a lunch to work is healthier, cheaper and faster than going out to eat for lunch. However, that does not solve the problem of how to make taking your lunch taste better!

In this section, I've included several tasty sandwich ideas to help you get excited for lunchtime – even if you are dining in! The recipe for *Peanut Chicken Pitas* (page 88) is fresh, light and delicious! It is easy to prepare ahead so you are ready to grab and go in the morning. The *Turkey Avocado Pinwheels* (page 91) are another favorite at the Tilley house! You can see from the nutritional information, these are not only easy on your pocketbook, but also on your waistline.

One of the common behaviors I see when counseling patients is that they eat too few calories at breakfast and lunch causing them to overeat in the evening. Here is a good guide for how to make certain you are balancing your brown bag lunch by including foods that give you all the nutrients and fiber you need to be healthy and energetic until afternoon snack. This lunch provides about 400 calories which is a good target for the average adult trying to maintain a healthy weight. If you need to lose weight, eliminate one slice of bread and eat everything else on the list.

Lunch:
2 slices of whole wheat bread
1 oz lean turkey breast
1 oz low-fat cheese slice
2 slices avocado
1 tablespoon honey Dijon mustard
1 cup of baby carrots, cherry tomatoes, cucumber slices
1 small apple

BARBEQUED SALMON SANDWICHES

Ingredients

4 (5 oz.) salmon fillets

1 teaspoon McCormick's Spicy Montreal Steak Seasoning

½ cup Chipotle BBQ sauce

4 hot dog buns, preferably egg or brioche-style buns, toasted

1 cup prepared coleslaw

Directions

1. Preheat grill, brush lightly with olive oil. Sprinkle salmon fillets with steak seasoning. Brush each fillet with 1 tablespoon BBQ sauce. Place salmon top side down and grill over medium heat for 5 minutes. Gently turn fillets and cook additional 5 minutes or to desired degree of doneness.

2. Remove fillets from grill, leaving skin on grate. Place each piece of salmon on bun, top with coleslaw and drizzle evenly with remaining ¼ cup BBQ sauce.

Makes 4 servings

Nutrition Information

370 calories, 11 grams fat, 70 mg cholesterol, 1120 mg sodium, 30 grams carbohydrate, 2 gram fiber, 34 grams protein

Exchanges: 2 carbohydrate, 5 protein, 2 fat

Ingredients

2 cups cooked chicken, diced

½ cup spicy peanut sauce

8 large lettuce leaves

1 cup cooked whole grain noodles

1 cup shredded carrots

1 cup diced cucumbers

¼ cup chopped peanuts

Directions

1. In medium bowl, combine chicken and peanut sauce. Cover with plastic wrap and microwave for 1 minute; set aside.

2. In each lettuce leaf layer noodles, chicken, carrots, cucumbers and peanuts.

3. Roll (like a burrito), eat & enjoy.

   Makes 4 servings (2 each)

Nutrition Information

220 calories, 7 grams fat, 50 mg cholesterol, 150 mg sodium,
17 grams carbohydrate, 4 grams fiber, 23 grams protein

Exchanges: 1 carbohydrate, 3 protein, 1 fat

FRENCH DIP SANDWICHES

Ingredients

3 pounds boneless rump roast, trimmed of all fat

6 garlic cloves

5 teaspoons low-sodium beef bouillon granules

½ cup cider vinegar

4 low-sodium beef bouillon cubes

1-½ cups water

8 hoagie buns

Directions

1. Stick garlic cloves into roast, and place in slow cooker. Sprinkle with beef granules. Cover with vinegar. Cook on low for 8 hours or overnight. Do not uncover while cooking.

2. Remove roast and slice or pull apart, keep warm.

3. Strain juice into saucepan; add bouillon cubes and water, bring to a boil.

4. To serve, place sliced beef on hoagie buns. Place au jus in small bowls and serve with sandwiches.

   Makes 12 servings

Nutrition Information

290 calories, 8 grams fat, 70 mg cholesterol, 270 mg sodium, 24 grams carbohydrate, 1 gram fiber, 30 grams protein

Exchanges: 1.5 carbohydrate, 4 protein, 1.5 fat

Ingredients

½ cup low fat mayonnaise

¼ cup chopped green chilies, undrained

2 cloves garlic, chopped

2 tablespoons pickled jalapeno peppers, finely chopped

2 tablespoons chopped fresh cilantro

1-¼ pounds lean ground beef

1 teaspoon McCormick's Steak Seasoning

4 (1 oz) slices reduced-fat Colby Jack cheese

4 whole grain hamburger buns

Directions

1. Process mayonnaise, green chilies and garlic in food processor until smooth. Place in medium bowl and stir in jalapeno peppers and cilantro. Cover and refrigerate while preparing burgers.

2. Shape ground beef into 4 burgers. Season each burger with steak seasoning. Grill, turning once, for about 10 minutes, or to desired doneness. Top burgers with cheese and cook until cheese is melted.

3. Toast buns on grill. Place burger on bottom half of bun. Spread about 2 tablespoons of green chili mayonnaise on top half. Place on top of burger and serve. May serve remainder of mayonnaise in small bowl for dipping.

Makes 4 servings

Nutrition Information (burger, bun & 2 T mayo)

390 calories, 16 grams fat, 95 mg cholesterol, 790 mg sodium, 25 grams carbohydrate, 35 grams protein

Exchanges: 1.5 carbohydrate, 5 protein, 3 fat

Ingredients

6 skinless, boneless chicken breasts

1 cup teriyaki sauce

6 slices pineapple

6 slices reduced-fat Swiss cheese

6 whole wheat hamburger buns

1 red onion, sliced

6 red leaf lettuce leaves

½ cup Marzetti Coleslaw Dressing

Directions

1. Place chicken breasts in large Ziplock bag, pour in teriyaki sauce, and seal; marinate at least 8 hours or overnight.

2. Remove chicken from bag and discard marinade. Grill over medium heat for about 5 minutes on each side or until done.

3. During last 2 minutes of cooking time, place pineapple slices on grill, turning once. Top each chicken breast with cheese slice.

4. To serve, place cheese topped chicken breast on bun, top with pineapple slice, onion slice, and lettuce – drizzle with coleslaw dressing and enjoy!

Makes 6 servings

Nutrition Information

440 calories, 17 grams fat, 85 mg cholesterol, 660 mg sodium, 39 grams carbohydrate, 4 grams fiber, 37 grams protein

Exchanges: 2.5 carbohydrate, 5 protein, 3 fat

Ingredients

1 (3 pound) boneless rump roast, trimmed of all visible fat

2 medium onions

1 (12 oz) can Coca-Cola (not diet)

⅓ cup Worcestershire sauce

1-½ tablespoons apple cider vinegar

1-½ teaspoons beef bouillon granules

¾ teaspoon each dry mustard and chili powder

¼ to ½ teaspoon ground cayenne pepper

2 cloves garlic, minced

1 cup ketchup

12 whole wheat hamburger buns

Directions

1. Place roast in a 3-½ or 4 quart electric slow cooker; add onion.

2. In medium bowl, combine cola, Worcestershire sauce, vinegar, beef granules, dry mustard, chili powder, cayenne pepper and minced garlic. Reserve and chill 1 cup sauce. Pour remaining sauce over roast.

3. Cover and cook on high 6 hours or on low 9 hours until roast is very tender. Remove roast from cooker and shred meat.

4. Combine reserved sauce and ketchup in a saucepan; cook over medium heat, stirring constantly, until thoroughly heated. Pour sauce over shredded meat, stirring gently. Spoon meat mixture onto buns.

Makes 12 servings

Nutrition Information

310 calories, 7 grams fat, 50 mg cholesterol, 650 mg sodium, 34 grams carbohydrate, 2 grams fiber, 26 grams protein

Exchanges: 2 carbohydrate, 4 protein, 1 fat

PEANUT CHICKEN PITAS

Ingredients

4 cups romaine lettuce leaves, torn into bite-size pieces

2 cups chopped cooked chicken breast

¾ cup snow peas, cut into ½" slices

¼ cup shredded carrots

¼ cup chopped roasted lightly salted peanuts

⅓ cup light sesame-ginger dressing

4 whole wheat pita sandwich rounds, halved

Directions

1. Combine chopped lettuce and next 4 ingredients in a large bowl. Drizzle with sesame-ginger dressing; toss to combine.

2. Fill each pita half evenly with mixture.

   Makes 4 servings (2 halves)

Nutrition Information

160 calories, 5 grams fat, 40 mg cholesterol, 240 mg sodium, 12 grams carbohydrate, 2 grams fiber, 17 grams protein

Exchanges: 1 carbohydrate, 2.5 protein, 1 fat

SOUTHWEST BEEF WRAPS

Ingredients

4 large whole wheat flour tortillas

½ cup black bean dip

12 oz. thinly sliced peppered deli roast beef

½ cup mashed avocado

½ cup chunky salsa

1 cup reduced-fat shredded pepper jack cheese

Directions

1. To prepare wraps, make an assembly line with the ingredients. Spread each tortilla with ¼ of each ingredient: start with bean dip, add beef, avocado, salsa and cheese.

2. Roll up like a burrito and wrap in plastic wrap. Place in refrigerator until ready to pack in lunchbox.

   Makes 4 servings

Nutrition Information

400 calories, 14 grams fat, 55 mg cholesterol, 1180 mg sodium, 33 grams carbohydrate, 5 grams fiber, 32 grams protein

Exchanges: 2 carbohydrate, 4.5 protein, 3 fat

Ingredients

1 small cucumber, peeled and thinly sliced

1 teaspoon each vinegar and canola oil

Dash of black pepper and dried whole dill weed

1 (6 oz) can albacore tuna (in water), drained and flaked

½ cup chopped celery

¼ cup light mayonnaise

12 slices thin sliced whole wheat bread

2 hard-boiled eggs, sliced thin

Directions

1. Combine cucumber, vinegar, oil, pepper and dill weed, tossing well. Cover and chill while preparing rest of sandwich.

2. Combine tuna, celery and mayonnaise; mix well; set aside.

3. Toast bread on both sides. Spread tuna mixture on 4 toasted slices; top with another toasted slice. Layer ¼ of the egg slices and ¼ of the cucumber slices on top of each toast slice. Top with remaining toast slices. Cut each sandwich in half diagonally; secure with wooden pick. Serve immediately.

Makes 4 servings

Nutrition Information

270 calories, 8 grams fat, 125 mg cholesterol, 650 mg sodium, 34 grams carbohydrate, 11 grams fiber, 21 grams protein

Exchanges: 2 carbohydrate, 3 protein, 1.5 fat

TURKEY AVOCADO PINWHEELS

Ingredients

6 low carb whole wheat tortilla wraps

¾ cup Ken's Light Honey Mustard Dressing

1 avocado, sliced thin

3 slices bacon, cooked and crumbled

6 romaine lettuce leaves, chopped

1 pound peppered turkey breast, shaved

Directions

1. Spread each tortilla with 2 tablespoons of dressing. Layer each tortilla evenly with avocado, bacon, lettuce and turkey.

2. Fold edges of tortillas over layers and roll tightly.

   Makes 6 servings

Nutrition Information

370 calories, 14 grams fat, 30 mg cholesterol, 800 mg sodium, 28 grams carbohydrate, 4 grams fiber, 19 grams protein

Exchanges: 2 carbohydrate, 3 protein, 3 fat

Roasted Fresh Asparagus, p. 100

Side Dishes

Side dishes are a fantastic way to build more nutrients into your diet. When you accompany a dish with brightly colored vegetables and whole grains, you are adding minimal calories and maximum nutrition!

Be aware of the difference between starchy and non-starchy vegetables. The starchy ones – like potatoes, corn, green peas and sweet potatoes – have more carbohydrates and calories than non-starchy vegetables. Both are nutrient rich (full of vitamins, minerals, antioxidants and fiber). Feel free to fill-up on the non-starchy variety like broccoli, carrots, zucchini and tomatoes – these are only 25 calories per ½ cup while starchy veggies have about 80 calories per ½ cup.

The recipe in this section for *Mashed Maple Sweet Potatoes* (page 98) is amazing served with pork or chicken. Sweet potatoes are an excellent source of beta-carotene and vitamin A which act as antioxidants and help maintain healthy vision.

I've included a recipe for *Roasted Asparagus* (page 100) - it is super simple, but is, in my humble opinion, the most delicious way to prepare asparagus! Asparagus is a non-starchy vegetable and is a great source of vitamin K, folate, and vitamin C. Vitamin K is an essential component for helping your blood clot when you're injured. Folate is important for cell growth. Vitamin C is an effective antioxidant that keeps your body healthy. Isn't it amazing that something with only 25 calories per ½ cup serving can do so many wonderful things for your body?

CARAMELIZED CAULIFLOWER

Ingredients

1 lb. cleaned cauliflower florets

1 tablespoon extra virgin olive oil

¼ teaspoon each salt and pepper

Directions

1. Toss cauliflower in large bowl with oil, salt and pepper.
2. Place on 10x15-inch jelly roll pan (cookie sheet with sides).
3. Roast at 400 degrees, for about 15 minutes, stopping to stir every 5 minutes to prevent burning, until cauliflower is lightly browned.

   Makes 6 servings

Nutrition Information

40 calories, 2.5 grams fat, 0 mg cholesterol, 20 mg sodium,
4 grams carbohydrate, 2 grams fiber, 2 grams protein

Exchanges: 0 carbohydrate, 0.5 protein, 0.5 fat

Ingredients

4 cups new potatoes, cut into cubes

1 onion, diced

2 slices bacon, cooked and crumbled

2 tablespoons diced jalapenos

1 tablespoon butter

½ teaspoon each salt and pepper

1 cup low-fat cheddar cheese shreds

½ cup reduced-fat sour cream

Directions

1. On large piece of heavy-duty aluminum foil, layer potatoes, onion, bacon crumbles, and diced jalapenos. Top with butter and seasonings. Seal packet and place on grill over indirect heat for about 45 minutes or until potatoes are tender.* Gently shake packet 2 to 3 times during the cooking process to ensure even cooking.

2. Carefully open packet, pour into large bowl. Top with cheese and sour cream. Gently stir and place in serving bowl.

   *Can be baked in 400 degree oven for 40 to 45 minutes, instead of placing on grill.
   Makes 4 servings

Nutrition Information

270 calories, 10 grams fat, 30 mg cholesterol, 580 mg sodium, 33 grams carbohydrate, 4 grams fiber, 13 grams protein

Exchanges: 2 carbohydrate, 2 protein, 2 fat

FRESH TOMATO & SQUASH TART

Ingredients

1 large zucchini

1 large yellow squash

1 large potato, peeled

½ cup chopped onion

1 cup low-fat Swiss cheese, shredded, divided

2 eggs, lightly beaten

1 teaspoon salt

½ teaspoon Italian seasoning

¼ teaspoon ground black pepper

2 large tomatoes, thinly sliced

Directions

1. Spray a 9-inch pie plate with cooking spray; set aside.

2. Cut zucchini, summer squash and potato in half lengthwise; thinly slice crosswise and place all in large bowl. Stir in onion, ¾ cup Swiss cheese shreds, eggs, salt, Italian seasoning and pepper.

3. Arrange half of the tomato slices on bottom of pie plate. Evenly spoon vegetable mixture over tomatoes, pressing slightly to flatten. Arrange remaining tomato slices on top; sprinkle with remaining ¼ cup cheese.

4. Bake in a 400 degree oven until vegetables are tender; about 40 minutes.

Makes 6 servings

Nutrition Information

110 calories, 2.5 grams fat, 80 mg cholesterol, 480 mg sodium, 14 grams carbohydrate, 2 grams fiber, 9 grams protein

Exchanges: 1 carbohydrate, 1 protein, 0.5 fat

Ingredients

2 pounds sweet potatoes

¼ cup butter

½ cup firmly packed brown sugar

½ cup orange juice

1 cup fresh cranberries

Directions

1. Peel potatoes, and cut into large cubes. Cover with water, and bring to a boil. Cover, reduce heat, and simmer for 10 to 12 minutes or until just tender. Drain well, and set aside.

2. In large skillet, melt butter. Add potatoes and toss to coat. Stir in brown sugar, orange juice, and cranberries. Reduce heat and simmer for 10 minutes, stirring occasionally.

   Makes 8 servings

Nutrition Information

170 calories, 6 grams fat, 15 mg cholesterol, 75 mg sodium, 29 grams carbohydrates, 3 grams fiber, 1 grams protein

Exchanges: 2 carbohydrate, 0 protein, 1 fat

MASHED MAPLE SWEET POTATOES

Ingredients

2 pounds sweet potatoes, scrubbed

3 tablespoons butter

3 tablespoons maple syrup

½ teaspoon orange zest

½ teaspoon balsamic vinegar

½ teaspoon salt

½ teaspoon freshly ground black pepper

Directions

1. Preheat oven to 400 degrees. Pierce sweet potatoes with fork. Bake for 45 to 60 minutes until tender. Cut potatoes in half, lengthwise. Hold potato with pot holder and scoop out flesh into bowl; set aside.

2. In a medium saucepan, heat butter, syrup, zest and vinegar over medium-high heat. Remove from heat, add sweet potatoes and mash in pan with butter mixture. Season with salt and pepper. Serve immediately.

   Makes 6 servings

Nutrition Information

210 calories, 6 grams fat, 15 mg cholesterol, 250 mg sodium, 38 grams carbohydrate, 5 grams fiber, 3 grams protein

Exchanges: 2.5 carbohydrate, 0.5 protein, 1 fat

Ingredients

½ cup onion, diced

1 tablespoon butter

3 medium yellow squash, sliced

1 cup water

¼ cup salsa

¼ cup Velveeta Light, cubed

Directions

1. In medium saucepan, sauté onion in butter until translucent. Stir in squash and about 1 cup of water. Cover and cook over medium heat for about 10 minutes.

2. Drain well, add salsa and cheese and cook over low heat until heated through and cheese is melted.

   Makes 4 servings

Nutrition Information

100 calories, 4.5 grams fat, 15 mg cholesterol, 310 mg sodium,
10 grams carbohydrate, 2 grams fiber, 5 grams protein

Exchanges: 1 carbohydrate, 1 protein, 1 fat

Ingredients

1 pound fresh asparagus

2 tablespoons olive oil

½ teaspoon kosher salt

½ teaspoon fresh ground black pepper

Directions

1. Preheat oven to 400 degrees.

2. Break off tough ends of asparagus. Place on baking sheet with sides, drizzle with olive oil, toss gently to coat the asparagus. Spread in single layer and sprinkle with salt and pepper.

3. Place in oven for about 15 minutes; using spatula to stir asparagus every 5 minutes to ensure even roasting.

   Makes 4 servings

Nutrition Information

90 calories, 7 grams fat, 0 mg cholesterol, 230 mg sodium, 5 grams carbohydrate, 2 grams fiber, 3 grams protein

Exchanges: 0 carbohydrate, 0.5 protein, 1.5 fat

Ingredients

1 tablespoon olive oil

1 medium onion, sliced

3 medium zucchini, sliced

2 fresh tomatoes, sliced

1 tablespoon minced fresh basil

½ teaspoon garlic salt

¼ teaspoon pepper

½ cup dry stuffing mix

½ cup grated Parmesan cheese

¾ cup shredded reduced-fat cheddar cheese

Directions

1. In a large skillet, sauté onion in 1 tablespoon oil until crisp tender. Add zucchini and sauté for 2 minutes. Remove from heat and gently stir in tomatoes, basil, garlic, salt and pepper.

2. Place zucchini mixture in 1-½ quart baking dish. Top with stuffing mix; sprinkle with Parmesan cheese.

3. Cover and bake at 350 degrees for 20 minutes. Uncover and sprinkle with cheddar cheese. Return to the oven for 10 minutes or until golden.

Makes 8 servings

Nutrition Information

140 calories, 5 grams fat, 5 mg cholesterol, 570 mg sodium,
16 grams carbohydrate, 3 grams fiber, 9 grams protein

Exchanges: 1 carbohydrate, 1 protein, 1 fat

Sunkist Sherbet, p. 114

Desserts & Snacks

As a registered dietitian, I counsel hundreds of patients a year on how to build a healthy, balanced diet. I find that people generally fall into one of two camps – either they crave sweet or salty treats. Did you know that both can fit into a healthy diet? **The key is moderation!**

I've included some amazing recipes in this section that will definitely tempt your taste buds. Fit them into your healthy diet by enjoying a small amount. Healthy eating doesn't mean you can never enjoy dessert again – it simply means watch your portion!

One of our family favorites, and one of my most requested recipes, is *Strawberry Fluff* (page 113). The two secrets to a delicious fluff - be sure to beat the egg whites to a stiff peak, gently fold in the whipped cream and then let it freeze for a full 8 hours before serving. You are in for a decadent taste treat with this one!

If you are looking for a fun snack treat to make with your children, try the *Bird's Nests* (page 105). Shredded wheat biscuits, yogurt and fresh fruit make this a nutritious AND delicious snack. Kids love making them and the whole family will enjoy eating them!

The *All Bran Muffins* (page 104) are a wonderful breakfast treat. Keep them mixed in the refrigerator for up to 6 weeks, and make a fresh batch of muffins as you need them. Wow! They are amazing!

Did you know...

- Sweet and salty snacks are often full of carbohydrates which give your body quick energy, then can leave you feeling fatigued. Avoid this by adding a protein or healthy fat – like nuts – to slow the metabolism of the carbohydrate and thus prevent that sluggish feeling.
- For a light dessert, try fresh fruit topped with a dollop of yogurt sprinkled with sliced almonds or a small dip of light ice cream topped with a drizzle of light chocolate syrup and chopped pecans.
- For a savory snack, try *Spicy Nut Popcorn* (page 111). It is full of fiber and heart healthy fat – plus it is easy to transport AND delicious!

Ingredients

4 cups all bran cereal

2 cups bran flakes

2 cups boiling water

1 cup canola oil

2 cups sugar

4 eggs

5 cups flour

5 teaspoons baking soda

1 teaspoon salt

1 quart buttermilk

Directions

1. In very large bowl, combine bran cereals. Pour boiling water over the cereal; set aside.

2. In medium bowl, whisk together oil, sugar and eggs. Add to the bran mixture.

3. In medium bowl, combine all dry ingredients. Add the dry mixture (in small portions) alternately with buttermilk to the bran mixture. Stir just until all ingredients are moistened.

4. Spoon into greased 12-count muffin tin and bake at 400 degrees for 20 minutes or until firm in center.

5. Cover remaining mixture tightly and store in the refrigerator. It will keep for up to 6 weeks.

   Makes 48 servings

Nutrition Information

150 calories, 6 grams fat, 20 mg cholesterol, 230 mg sodium, 24 grams carbohydrate, 2 grams fiber, 3 grams protein

Exchanges: 1.5 carbohydrate, 0.5 protein, 1 fat

BIRD'S NESTS

Ingredients

8 shredded wheat biscuits (not mini)

⅓ cup brown sugar, packed

⅓ cup butter, melted

1 pint strawberries, sliced

1 apple, chopped

1 nectarine or peach, chopped

1 cup seedless grapes

1 cup low-fat vanilla yogurt

1 banana, peeled and sliced

Directions

1. Crumble the biscuits in a medium bowl; stir in brown sugar and butter.

2. Place ⅓ cup of biscuit mixture into each of 12 ungreased muffin cups and firmly press in bottom and up sides to make a "nest".

3. Bake at 350 degrees for 10 minutes; remove and let cool for 15 to 20 minutes.

4. In large bowl, mix together all fruit, except banana.

5. Fill the nest with the fruit mixture, top with a spoonful of vanilla yogurt and garnish with a banana slice.

   Makes 12 servings

Nutrition Information

160 calories, 5 grams fat, 15 mg cholesterol, 55 mg sodium, 27 grams carbohydrate, 3 grams fiber, 3 grams protein

Exchanges: 2 carbohydrate, 0.5 protein, 1 fat

BLACKBERRY APPLE CRISP WITH NUT TOPPING

Ingredients

3 Rome apples – peeled, cored and sliced ¼ inch thick

1-½ cups fresh blackberries

¼ cup granulated sugar

2 tablespoons all-purpose flour

Topping

½ cup all-purpose flour

⅓ cup rolled oats

⅓ cup whole almonds and pecans, coarsely chopped

3 tablespoons light brown sugar

½ teaspoon ground cinnamon

3 tablespoons butter

Directions

1. Preheat the oven to 350 degrees. Spray an 8 X 8-inch glass baking dish.

2. In a bowl, toss the apples with the blackberries, sugar and 2 tablespoons of flour. Spoon the filling into the baking dish.

3. In a small bowl, toss 1/2 cup of flour, oats, nuts, brown sugar and cinnamon. Add the butter and cut into flour mixture. Sprinkle the topping over the filling and bake for 35 minutes, until the filling is bubbling and the topping is browned. Let cool for 10 minutes before serving.

Makes 6 servings

Nutrition Information

240 calories, 10 grams fat, 15 mg cholesterol, 40 mg sodium, 36 grams carbohydrate, 4 grams fiber, 4 grams protein

Exchanges: 2.5 carbohydrate, 1 protein, 2 fat

CHERRY CRUNCH PARFAITS

Ingredients

2 tablespoons butter

¼ cup almonds, chopped

1 teaspoon cinnamon

8 commercial oatmeal cookies, crumbled

3 cups light vanilla ice cream, softened

1 (21 oz) can light cherry pie filling

Directions

1. Melt butter in skillet over low heat; add almonds, cinnamon and cookie crumbs. Set aside to cool.

2. Layer ½ of ice cream, crumb mixture, and pie filling evenly into six parfait glasses; repeat layers. Serve immediately.

Makes 6 servings

Nutrition Information

360 calories, 13 grams fat, 20 mg cholesterol, 220 mg sodium, 53 grams carbohydrate, 4 grams fiber, 7 grams protein

Exchanges: 3.5 carbohydrate, 1 protein, 2.5 fat

MAGIC CHERRY COBBLER

Ingredients

½ cup butter

1 cup all-purpose flour

¾ cup sugar

2 teaspoons baking powder

½ cup 1% milk

1 (14.5 oz) can red tart cherries in water, drained

½ cup sugar

Directions

1. Melt butter in an 8 X 8-inch Pyrex baking dish. Set aside.

2. Combine flour, ¾ cup sugar, and baking powder; add milk and stir until well blended. Spoon batter over butter in baking dish; do not stir.

3. Spoon cherries over batter. Sprinkle top with ½ cup sugar. Do not stir. Bake at 350 degrees for 45 minutes.

    Makes 8 servings

Nutrition Information

300 calories, 12 grams fat, 30 mg cholesterol, 150 mg sodium, 48 grams carbohydrate, 1 gram fiber, 3 grams protein

Exchanges: 3 carbohydrate, 0.5 protein, 2 fat

"NO-COOK" BANANA PUDDING

Ingredients

1 (14 oz) can fat-free Eagle Brand Milk

1-½ cups water

1 (3 oz) package instant vanilla pudding

1 (8 oz) container light whipped topping

3 bananas, sliced

30 vanilla wafers

6-8 maraschino cherries, optional

Directions

1. Blend together Eagle Brand Milk and water.

2. Add pudding and mix well. Place mixture in refrigerator and chill thoroughly.

3. Fold in whipped topping, and place ⅓ of pudding mixture in a glass bowl.

4. Add half of the bananas. Layer with half of vanilla wafers. Repeat layers and top with remaining pudding mixture.

5. Garnish with extra vanilla wafers and maraschino cherries, if desired.

   Makes 12 servings

Nutrition Information

260 calories, 4 grams fat, 5 mg cholesterol 220 mg sodium, 52 grams carbohydrate, 1 gram fiber, 4 grams protein

Exchanges: 3.5 carbohydrate, 1 protein, 1 fat

PINEAPPLE ANGEL CAKE

Ingredients

1 (14.5 oz) angel food cake mix

1 (20 oz) crushed pineapple, undrained

1 (12 oz) container
light whipped topping

2 (8 oz) cans crushed pineapple, drained

¼ cup chopped maraschino cherries

Directions

1. Grease and flour 9 X 13-inch baking pan.

2. In large bowl, beat together dry cake mix and 20 oz can of pineapple (with juice) for one minute.

3. Pour into prepared baking pan, and bake at 350 degrees for 30 minutes.

4. While baking, stir together frosting in medium bowl by combining whipped topping, 2 (8 oz) cans drained pineapple, and maraschino cherries. When cake is cool, top with whipped topping mixture and refrigerate.

Makes 16 servings

Nutrition Information

196 calories, 3 grams fat, 0 mg cholesterol, 290 mg sodium, 38 grams carbohydrate, 0 grams fiber, 3 grams protein

Exchanges: 2.5 carbohydrate, 0.5 protein, 0.5 fat

SPICY NUT POPCORN

Ingredients

2 tablespoons butter

½ cup pecans, coarsely chopped

½ cup slivered almonds

1 teaspoon chili powder

½ teaspoon salt

½ teaspoon grated lime peel

1 tablespoon fresh lime juice

¼ teaspoon ground cloves

¼ teaspoon pepper

24 cups air-popped popcorn

Directions

1. Melt butter in a large skillet over medium heat; add pecans and almonds and sauté 3 to 4 minutes. Stir in remaining ingredients (except popcorn) and heat through.

2. Pour warm mixture over popcorn, tossing to coat.

Makes 8 servings

Nutrition Information

210 calories, 13 grams fat, 10 mg cholesterol, 170 mg sodium, 21 grams carbohydrate, 5 grams fiber, 5 grams protein

Exchanges: 1.5 carbohydrate, 1 protein, 2.5 fat

Ingredients

1 (.6 oz) package Sugar Free Strawberry-Flavored Jell-O

1 cup boiling water

1 cup frozen sliced strawberries

1 (8 oz) container light whipped topping

1 (9-inch) graham cracker crust

Garnish with additional whipped topping and fresh strawberries, if desired

Directions

1. Dissolve gelatin in boiling water, add frozen strawberries, stirring well.

2. Chill until slightly jelled. Fold in whipped topping. Spoon into crust. Chill for at least 4 hours.

3. To serve, garnish with a dollop of whipped topping and sliced fresh strawberries, if desired.

   Makes 8 servings

Nutrition Information

230 calories, 11 grams fat, 0 grams cholesterol, 250 mg sodium, 30 grams carbohydrate, 1 gram fiber, 2 grams protein

Exchanges: 2 carbohydrate, 0.5 protein, 2 fat

STRAWBERRY FLUFF

Ingredients

1 cup all-purpose flour

¼ cup packed brown sugar

½ cup chopped pecans

½ cup unsalted butter

1 (10 oz) package sweetened frozen strawberries, thawed

2 egg whites

1 cup sugar

1 teaspoon vanilla extract

1 cup heavy whipping cream

Directions

1. To prepare crust: In medium bowl, combine flour, brown sugar, pecans and butter. Mix together with pastry cutter to form small crumbs.

2. Spray a large cookie sheet with cooking spray and spread the crust mixture out evenly. Bake at 400 degrees for 12-15 minutes; stirring often to brown crumb mixture; set aside to cool. Place three-fourths of mixture into 9 x 13-inch baking dish; pat to form crust. Reserve remaining crumbs for topping.

3. To prepare filling: In large mixing bowl, combine strawberries with juice, egg whites, sugar and vanilla. Beat at highest speed of electric mixer for 10 to 12 minutes; until stiff peaks form; set aside.

4. In small bowl, whip cream. Gently fold into strawberry mixture. Spread filling evenly over cooled crumb mixture. Sprinkle with remaining crumbs. Cover and place in freezer for 8 hours or overnight. Cut into squares and serve.

   Makes 18 servings

Nutrition Information

210 calories, 12 grams fat, 30 mg cholesterol, 10 mg sodium, 24 grams carbohydrate, 1 gram fiber, 2 grams protein

Exchanges: 1.5 carbohydrate, 0.5 protein, 2 fat

Ingredients

1 (14 oz) can fat-free sweetened condensed milk

4 (12 oz) cans orange Sunkist soda pop

1 (20 oz) can crushed pineapple

⅓ cup maraschino cherries, chopped

Directions

1. Combine condensed milk, orange soda, pineapple, and cherries into 6 quart ice cream freezer container and freeze according to manufacturer's instructions.

2. Pack freezer with additional rock salt and ice and let ripen 1 hour before serving.

   Makes 24 (½ cup) servings

Nutrition Information

90 calories, 0 grams fat, 0 mg cholesterol, 25 mg sodium, 22 grams carbohydrate, 0 grams fiber, 1 gram protein

Exchanges: 1.5 carbohydrate, 0 protein, 0 fat